T

FREE

ALTERNATIVE

000204

THE
FREELANCE
ALTERNATIVE

Marianne Gray

PIATKUS

AKNOWLEDGEMENTS

I would like to thank John Bridge of Southampton Technical College, Glynis Young of Sheffield University, Nick Bradley and Paul Harrison for their support, Gill Cormode for her inspired editing, and Michael Dunne, without whom this book could never have seen the light of day.

© 1987 by Marianne Gray

First published in 1987 by
Judy Piatkus (Publishers) Limited,
5 Windmill Street, London W1

British Library Cataloguing in Publication Data

Gray, Marianne
The freelance alternative.
1. Small business——Great Britain
2. Self-employed——Great Britain
I. Title
658'.041'0941   HD62.7

ISBN 0–86188–667–4
ISBN 0–86188–672–0 Pbk

Phototypeset in 10/12 pt Linotron Times by
Phoenix Photosetting, Chatham
Printed and bound in Great Britain by
Biddles Ltd, Guildford and King's Lynn

TO

**My Mother and Father who
taught me the value of independence**

CONTENTS

INTRODUCTION

This book has not been written for those who wistfully dream of going solo and running their own business, or even those who reckon they have a red-hot, infallible idea that would make them a million if only they had the time to do something about it. It is for those robust characters who can already hear the first grindings of wheels in motion, and those who have taken that first tantalising, sometimes traumatising, step along the road to a freelance life.

To many, breaking away from the world of bosses, salaries and office security has become the preferred alternative. Right now in Britain, more people are self-employed than at any time since the 1920s, with one in ten workers operating on this basis.

While many people who make the break would never dream of going back (or due to unemployment are not *able* to go back) to a regular job, many strike out on their own without giving sufficient thought to the middle-term future and then suddenly, shatteringly, find themselves washed up. With a little foresight and planning this should not happen.

I've tried to stick with the reality of working for yourself in this book. There isn't page after detailed page on tax or cashflow. Libraries have shelves of excellent books written by specialists on specialist subjects. Instead, I have concentrated on the less exposed aspects of being in charge of your own work, things like the psychology of functioning out there all on your own, organising a work and play routine that will suit your approach to life, and learning how to make the most of your assets, from self-promotion to emerging as a thriving economic force.

At the end, just for inspiration, I've thrown in a few dozen money-making ideas, in case you haven't yet managed to decide on your own solo project or future business empire.

PART ONE

1
THE LIE OF THE WORKING LAND

In the shrinking world of work the pattern of our lives has begun to change. The full-employment society most post-war children grew up with has gone and will not return. A worldwide shift to more and more temporary employment means that workers are having to adapt to fit the more flexible mould of the new labour market.

As such, this job revolution – a sort of modern version of the Industrial Revolution – is a dramatic turn of events. In the long term it will mean there will be no jobs for life; job security will be an outmoded concept that people who were employed used to enjoy. In the short term it will mean a quick revision of attitudes towards work and jobs. Whether we welcome it or not, new patterns of work are on their way.

Already the outlines of some of these changes are very clear. Increasingly we are accepting the part-time work society. Working practices are changing to secure greater flexibility across great trenches of British industry and commerce. There is growing evidence of industry declining and services expanding, and there is a definite swing from the huge sprawling corporates to more modest companies with a small core of personnel who use outside workers to perform specialist tasks.

This is the first link in a chain to achieve flexibility to meet new needs. The fact is that long-time staff workers are being replaced by short-contract outsiders who offer maximum adaptability in the workplace.

These outsiders, often working in the twilight zone on the edge of the Black Economy, sometimes form part of a network of freelancers. Often they are self-employed people who prefer to operate on their own. Sometimes they come in the form of partnerships and co-ops, small businesses or one-man bands. Many of them work part time. Some of them do several jobs concurrently. A lot of them work the proverbial self-employed 25-hour-day eight days a week. Some simply take on work when they have to, to top up funds.

This new working climate is exciting. There is a growing opportunity for people to reshape their working lives according to choice or inner impulse. You can live your life without a job as such, or have many jobs or many different bosses.

Many people have made a conscious decision to live outside the system as freelancers, preferring to create their own economic space while tapping their full potential as human beings. Others are forced to do this because they have young children to look after at home or are otherwise housebound. For some, being beyond the realms of the establishment is the only place they want to be, and the new population of unemployed who can no longer find any room within the system *have* to seek work further afield.

There have always been self-employed workers, and now, in Britain, their numbers are at their highest since 1926, when the country still prided itself on being a nation of small shopkeepers. Three out of four self-employed people would not change their lot even if they were offered comparable employment with similar earnings, working for an employer.

In 1984, according to the Labour Force Survey, some 2·6 million people were self-employed in their main job (11·2 per cent of all employment), a number that had grown by close on half a million in three years from 1981 to 1984. In 1986 it was nearing three million.

For a long time there was very little planning, legislation or political underpinning for this new work revolution developing quietly but steadily on the sidelines. Politicians either overlooked it or thought it must be a devious tax avoidance ploy. And for far too long the British, with their reputation for being good losers, had found it out of character to admit overtly to being ambitious and spiked with entrepreneurial desires. We trivialised achievement. Drive and the desire to make money was something only Americans had. Until recently it really was almost unthinkable to work for yourself. You were either employed or unemployed, and that was it. The 'employee mentality' discouraged initiative.

For much of this century business has not been fashionable in

Britain. The upper class considered it vulgar, the middle class preferred the respectability of the professions, and the working class saw itself locked in conflict with business. The combination of these attitudes has contributed to our industrial decline by impoverishing our business class over the years so that today it lacks the confidence, ability or status of its counterparts in America, Japan or West Germany.

But now, with one in eight out of work in the UK, the powers that be are realising that free enterprise is good for the economy and a blush of respectability is forming on the cheeks of the small business person. In some quarters it has become positively fashionable to be a solo worker. Suddenly, there are numerous outlets offering training, advice and funds and the government has introduced a broad range of measures to encourage the hesitant to make that decisive leap into business start-up.

Dr James Curran, Reader in Industrial Sociology at Kingston Polytechnic and author of a recent review on the role of the small enterprise in Britain's economy has said:

> *Since 1971 there has been an increasingly rapid expansion in the number of small enterprises in Britain. In 1971 the Bolton Committee – the last official full-scale inquiry on the small business in Britain – offered a very pessimistic view but the picture has been almost totally reversed since. Now, virtually one in 12 of those at work are self-employed, and the work-force itself is roughly divided into three thirds: one third works in the public sector, one third works for large-scale private enterprises and one third works in the small business sector or in self-employment.*

However, I have found that not everybody is turning to self-employment with the same enthusiasm. Even the change in emphasis from manufacturing to service industries in the second half of the 20th century is hard to accept. Many people are enduring changes in their working lives – like unemployment – unwillingly, with unease and discomfort. They always loved being in a job and don't wish to become self-employed. The furthest thing from their minds would be to set up on their own.

For some who simply were not able to see what was going to happen and move with the tide, these changing work patterns have meant redundancy and unemployment. Others have seen their jobs go long before they were due to, courtesy of 'voluntary' early retirement. In some cases this might have proved to be a joyful gain of free time, but for others it has been the reality of being dumped on the scrapheap without warning and prematurely. Not everyone can adapt to discovering hobbies and the right to be lazy after a lifetime of work – work that they have probably lived, eaten, drunk and slept! So many of the people I see going through the Manpower Services Enterprise Allowance Scheme are middle-aged redundant executives who could no more consider retiring to do nothing than fly.

For others, like many school-leavers and university graduates who cannot even get a foot on the accepted work ladder, it will mean a total lack of incentive and direction into organised or gainful employment and possibly a generation that will never have the pleasure – or the burden – of a nine-to-five job.

Before examining the motivation behind wanting to work for yourself, it is fascinating to look at the reasons behind why people want to work at all. According to Dr Andrew Stanway, a psycho-sexual and marital physician and prominent author, most people tend to overlook the unconscious motives for work:

> *Earning a crust means very different things for men and for women. Work to men is a sort of sophisticated game. In the West it is the most important thing in a man's life. It can be a very seductive mistress. For a woman there is a totally different slant because she knows that she has a far more important job, creating the next generation. Work is not her main* raison d'être.
>
> *Making sense of your working life and the unconscious motives can take a lifetime. Consider some of the motives: fulfilling parental expectation; spouse pressure to work; outside pressure provided by something like feminism for women; the need to get out of the house and away from spouse and children; and that old favourite, guilt, like 'isn't it a waste of training' when a female brain surgeon who would rather be at home looking after her baby goes back to work.*

THE NEW APPROACH

Now, with the new more flexible approach to staff and working patterns, the job-for-life syndrome has to be completely rethought. The eight-hour day for five days a week for 49 weeks a year (or 48 or 50 depending on the employer) is already an anachronism in many places where the ideal of full-employment has been seen to be an impossibility.

At last the 'system' is gradually making noises about it being preferable to give everybody a job for part of their lives rather than give it to some for all of their lives and to some not at all. But how to do this has no clear blueprint yet. Self-employment and the creation of small businesses is only a fraction of the plan.

This change of emphasis in the world of work is by no means just Britain's problem. It is an international phenomenon. The International Labour Organisation (ILO) estimates that one thousand million new jobs would have to be created between now and the year 2000 to achieve full employment. While this statistic might be accurate, as I am sure it is, the concept is a somewhat dazzling one in this time of new workplace technology in the form of more and more sophisticated computers, networks, robots and other marvels of the electronic age.

Already technology has had a heavy impact on the way we work. Automation means less manpower. Hundreds of thousands of jobs in the manufacturing sector have been lost as Britain has become more of a service economy. In 1986, for the first time in our history, we imported more manufactured goods than we exported. In May 1987, the unemployed figure stood at a depressing 3,143,370, a figure mainly representing what is called technological unemployment. Our discovery of means of economising on the use of labour is outstripping the pace at which we find new uses for that labour.

The resilience of the work-force has clearly been weakened by lack of motivation and loss of heart. It can be a hard choice between being unemployed or self-employed, but a tough economic climate and a sense of survival have pushed many of those who are prepared to take the risk into creating their own work.

In Britain the decision to become self-employed is not the same as the desire to make a fortune. This is in marked contrast to the United States, where being an entrepreneur means little unless there is big money to be made. Here, it is a mixture of the desire to strike out alone and make your mark, to realise a bit of self-expression and to get on with life. People often wish to become self-employed for reasons of lifestyle and personal satisfaction as such as any financial motives. After all, to quote Robert Louis Stevenson, 'Every one lives by selling something.' It is not always necessary to sell more than is needed to have a pleasant life.

With 120,000 people going self-employed each year (Department of Employment figures), it is clearly a growing force. Unofficial figures, however, estimate that there are now between six and seven million self-employed in Britain, the majority of whom do not declare their small extra mural enterprises.

While it seems that Britain is experiencing a revitalisation of the small-business spirit, it doesn't mean a sudden shift to the other side of the work fence. Employed people have been moonlighting for years. Some have done it at night, after work, or at weekends. Others have done it in the boss's time, with the convenience of their office desk and free use of the telephone. When you're really on your own, even buying a paperclip is a capital investment!

A large proportion of the potential self-employed go solo with caution, choosing first to work as outworkers, part-timers or temporaries before cutting the cord and switching to total self-employment.

Few beginners in self-employment, apart from fired-up business-types and entrepreneurs, deliberately embark on the path of big risks involved in developing a growth business. Where possible they have the safety net of a part-time contract or the promise of small but regular pieces of paid work – which makes sense while it is impossible to anticipate fully the fiscal times ahead.

Part-time workers (those whom the Department of Employment considers work for less than 30 hours a week), in quantitative terms, are on the increase both in hours and bodies, preferring to work a little to joining the growing number of the forcibly idle. 'Employment' contracts embodying an increasing variety of terms and conditions are emerging for part-timers, for outworkers and for freelance 'consultants' as the 'flexible firm' finds its feet. At the time of writing the Institute of Manpower Studies is actively working for employment contracts for alternative workers.

The temporary staff market has also been swelling its ranks. According to Manpower, the temporary staff specialists, about two million people will *only* have temporary jobs in 1987, compared to 1.5 million in 1984.

A fair number of those temporary workers will be in the temp.

sec. mould. But there will also be a new breed of executive, the temp. exec., who is employed on a short contract on a highly specialised basis, to consult, troubleshoot, headhunt and sweep clean for a decent fee.

With the job-pattern changes and companies trimming their budgets, it makes far better financial sense for companies to hire in when needed. The professional they sub-contract – or out-source – to will most likely be well paid and well cared for in return for working where and when needed. He or she will be a flexi-worker in the full sense, operating in a flexible working environment. Says Ray Smith, director of the management consultants Inbucon:

Because companies have learned to be slim and to be profitable they want to keep their head count low, their fixed costs low. One route to doing this is to employ a senior staffer on a temporary basis. Our clients started approaching us to do this a few years ago and the service ran very fast indeed.

One recent case was when a firm took on an executive chairman who in a year turned a company that was losing money fast into a very successful business.

Something like this Rent-A-Boss attitude is the first real sign of truly socially acceptable self-employment. In the West where, generally speaking, most of us have grown up believing we'd have a job for life – more specifically, the job we trained to do as young adults (usually) at the prompting of parents and peers – it's a complete turnaround.

Our job, trade or profession used to be the most stable feature of our lives and we tended not to change it. Those who did change horses in mid-stream were often considered professionally unreliable. Now people are taking these jobs, trades and professions with them to strike out on their own, or changing course completely. This is something that will undoubtedly shape the rest of the century.

Fired executives are often bitten by the entrepreneurial bug. The more who are made redundant, the more the shift from manager to entrepreneur will grow. Already the manager is fast becoming an endangered species as many contemplate the move to freelancing.

Of course, one must not overlook the executive who dreads the day his redundancy papers come. Comments Erskine Small:

It will inevitably happen, but I must say I'm not wild about it.

For me it will probably mean having to be three times as efficient. I'm no entrepreneur. I enjoy getting into the office at ten, dictating a few letters, taking a client out to lunch till three and then driving home before the rush-hour sets in. I'd rather have a moderate salary and be a happy slouch with an office and a secretary than be a ground-breaker with the opportunity to earn more money and use my brain to the full.

While I parried that one with the comment that it was little wonder we are in the state we are in, another manager friend, stifled by the weight of office politics and bureaucracy, restored my hopes:

I can't wait to be given the golden handshake and get out to prove myself. Apart from anything, my morale needs boosting, my self-respect needs wheeling out for review. However, I'm not brave enough to quit now and give in my notice because if I wait a few more years I'll probably be made redundant and get all that lolly!

For the employer the new flexible system of out-sourcing to freelancers has proved very favourable. It is obviously cheaper as there are no overheads, tax, National Insurance or pensions to pay.

Rank Xerox reckon that each employee earning £10,000 p.a. costs them £12,000 in office overheads and a further £5,000 in costs such as National Insurance and pension. They actively encourage their staff to leave and set up their own businesses and then to work on a contract basis for Rank. This system has worked well for Rank, and it is also perfect for those staffers who wanted a bit more independence.

But this magic word 'flexibility' has worrying overtones given the ease with which employers can now replace short-contract staff. How magic it is will only be seen when a system and contracts are established that ensure protection for the flexible worker.

The sub-contracted person, unless he has something very special to offer, knows that there are many similar people out there who are probably just as good as he is. In a waning economy competition thrives. Among the self-employed, competition, for the person who risks tackling life on his or her own terms, is a motivating force. The keener, leaner self-employed person finds the pace brisk and stimulating. For them, there were extra plusses to their new-found independence that rested on the side of money. The tax system favoured them more than their salaried counterparts (to a certain extent) and they no longer were obliged to join trade unions.

Opting out

Today's self-employed have been backed up by the ageing 'baby boomers', the branch of the Work Family that went off in the 1960s to do its own thing. Born between 1946 and 1961 and heavily influenced by the era of peace, love and being laid back, they represented the prime-age work-force. A lot of them really did *not* want to be part of the corporate structure and they consistently opted out, at war with the System. They preferred to have jobs they could express themselves in and challenges to get their teeth into. They weren't prepared to let their ambitions be nipped in the bud – or the budget!

Gerald, 40, a City man 'gone bust', said:

> *Why sit through that tedious routine of taking orders and doing your expected workload in return for a cheque and severe soul-erosion, when you can get away and think it out for yourself? Many of us in those jobs can turn out to be really bright when left to our own devices. I have made a lot of money developing property for myself instead of developing invest-ments for somebody else.*
>
> *I've delegated much of the work now and have time to do what I always wanted to do, which is picture restoring. I have the time to do it, the money to foot my unavoidable bills and the space to do it in – I converted one of my properties into a workspace so I could have my own little studio and make an income from the rest of the building. It was just a matter of that hackneyed old saying about limits only existing in one's mind. My choices are limitless, or so I believe.*

The emergence of this group had a positive impact on self-employment. From the early 1970s they began to create their own independent jobs rather than join the squeeze. Having witnessed in the 1960s the awakening of public awareness of aspects of life like politics, the economy, corruption in high business and so on, they wanted no part of it.

Women, at that time, were already making a strong impression on the self-employed ranks. It was becoming acceptable, and often necessary, for wives and mothers to work. In America, women came to dominate the freelance movement. In Britain, they took nearly 50 per cent of the part-time and home-based jobs.

More and more people felt the need to leave the rat race and move away from the city and into something more spiritually edifying. Several of them were half-way there already by having been what is now called an intrepreneur, which is an entrepreneur *within* an organisation. Jerrard Stock, intrepreneur turned entrepreneur:

> *It's a difficult word to say and a difficult concept to explain. Working in a corporation you are supposed to resist new ideas officially but there are always a few people earmarked to be the intrepreneurs, the troubleshooters, the experimenters, who do the work and then the company claims the glory.*

Values changed. The traditional notion of security was superseded by independence with risk, and the freedom to choose. For the first time it was a matter of enthusiasm finding the opportunities and allowing energy to make the most of them. For these people, spending five days a week clawing their way up the corporate ladder while slaving for the greater glory of a faceless factory or corporation was totally unsatisfactory and pointless.

Being able to see a little further into the future and take the new opportunities appealed. The prospect of no layoffs, no commuting, no bosses, no hours, no wardrobe worries, no in-house politics and no childcare problems that come with working at home became very hard to resist! Family life improved as work improved.

They found, as we still do, that there are plenty of chances to change direction. Many people choose to do something they weren't doing when they were employed. It would, after all, be pointless for the redundant BP executive to keep to his former working style. BP could not exactly be described as a small business, and the ex-exec. would have to be prepared to make major alterations. Small businesses and large firms are different and it's a fallacy that if you can run a big business you can run a small one.

Some career changers today opt for old-fashioned work in the crafts like weaving, restoring, framing, pottery and enamelling. Some elect to work in service-based jobs like plumbing, tutoring and hairdressing. Those who can raise the cash dive into the thing they've always dreamed of doing. A few people from the media/arts world, like designers, journalists, model-makers and illustrators, can easily set up offices or studios in their second bedroom (or corner of the kitchen in some cases). Those from the top of the tree become consultants. Those who never wanted to be at the top settle into something that will never be quoted on the Stock Exchange.

Stimulated by adrenalin and charged with ambition, the free-lancers who successfully survive the first few years know that there is no way they'll be returning to the sheltered grind of employment. Freedom, various surveys have shown, is the strongest motivating force, and where there's freedom, money becomes the second most important factor. Anyway, one person's work is another person's leisure!

Ideally suited to the new, faster-moving sections of the economy – communications and high technology – freelancers find there's plenty of space on the work-front for them to fill. They don't suffer from work dissatisfaction. The more ambitious ones, after a degree of success, start to respond to the twitch and feel that they could do bigger and better things.

A generation of young entrepreneurs has burst on to the scene. People like Richard Branson with his Virgin empire, Anita Roddick of The Body Shop, Debbie Moore of The Dance Centre, Eddy Shah of *Today* fame. Most of them are not from Oxbridge, and many of them seem to be individuals who had problems with authority, or left school early with only an O-level or two to their name. They had a vision they had to pursue. They were self-made, alert, streetwise and wanting to go somewhere that hadn't been reached before.

'Entrepreneurs never find the world is quite right so they want to change it', comments Richard Branson, while Anita Roddick, her-self of Italian roots, describes them as people who 'think like an immigrant, out of step with society because they aren't part of it.'

Most self-employed people subscribe to the old-fashioned work ethic – which is just as well as frequently their characters mean they work harder than they would have had to as part of a corporate structure. While building up their businesses the majority of free-lancers work longer hours (an average of 55 hours a week with spouses/partners helping them on an average of 26 hours a week) and put up with earning less than their employed counterparts. Later, of course, work and income should level off as desired.

Dr Curran, however, sees the self-employed owner/manager running his business from a spider's web, with owner/manager in the centre, surviving each day/week/month as it comes. Instead of working to a five-year plan, today's self-employed owner/manager runs the business with impulsive managerial style and has difficulty delegating.

> *Small business owners are usually good at production, at producing the goods or service their enterprise is based on. Their major weaknesses are in finance and marketing. They often display the familiar 'numbers block' of the British. They are reluctant to borrow or to seek outside help from, for instance, venture capitalists because they believe it will mean they will lose control over the business. Equally, they often fail to market positively. They frequently feel that if you make a good product or offer a good service then people are bound to come to you anyway.*

The image of the harassed sole trader working late, knee-deep in government paperwork and red-tape, while struggling to achieve what is known as 'a positive cashflow', is not that far off the mark. From my experience, I put some of that down to traditional shortcomings like the stiff upper lip, which makes it difficult to ask for help when in dire need, and also the national feeling that the desire for riches and success is not really on. But these things, I'm sure, will be worked through by most freelancers! (See Chapter Six for more.)

Without a doubt the life-enhancing satisfaction of doing one's own thing outweighs everything else. That, combined with the knowledge that the more we do the more we make (there is no middle person or company to cream off the hard-earned profits), makes the illusion of security from an Establishment job pale.

The framework of self-employment is now sturdier than it was even five or ten years ago. However, for those in need, those pushed off the job ladder and squeezed out of the job market, with no target to keep in sight, taking the self-employed route will, for many, be an endurance test. With luck they will soon realise that there is no great barrier preventing people from being successful in business. Like most things it's a question of risking the prospect of defeat for the chance of achieving excellence.

Running a business makes large demands and not everyone is equipped to do it (see Chapter Three to check your score). It is a matter of the survival of the fittest. Today there is so much information, training and help available to minimise the element of risk that nobody can excuse themselves by saying they didn't know what was ahead. The self-employed route is not easy, but it is exciting. It can be difficult, but it is always different. I honestly do not know any self-employed person who would even consider returning to employee status.

Most self-employed people find – or come to find – that self-employment is a calling rather than a job. Work is more than a job. It can contribute a lot to our quality of life. This is especially true for the individual who is in control of their piece of the action.

The dream of self-employment seems to be turning into reality. The traditional blue- and white-collar hierarchy, the tired face of work, needs a face-lift, and the freelancers are the people who will give it one, wearing whatever colour collar they like.

2
WHAT IS FREELANCING ALL ABOUT?

What freelancing is

The first question that crosses the mind of anybody who is idly thinking of switching to freelancing will be 'What's it all about?'

The self-employed, once converted, tend to move swiftly into the freelance world, letting their links with 'normal' working folk slip. This is a natural change brought about by new circumstances that I'll go into later. The point I want to make here is that it is difficult – sometimes impossible – to find out from a self-employed person exactly *what* being self-employed is all about.

Most of them will murmur about cashflow, the joy of working for yourself, aims, ideas, independence and freedom of choice. And the bottom line – making a profit, of course, and paying the bills. But the pursuit of money is not what usually motivates the free-lancer. It's the business of excellence, the pursuit of that dominant force, the vision, what really pushes them on.

This position is all very well when examined in context, but without full expansion it is tough to get a picture of what self-employment has to offer.

It certainly offers all that they say. It also offers a completely new lifestyle, nothing like the lifestyle you will have experienced as a nine-to-fiver, nothing like the lifestyle conventional schooling has geared you for, and not a lot like the lifestyle that has existed in Britain since the start of the Industrial Revolution.

The freelance lifestyle reaches far beyond the framework of work as the employee knows it. People in regular employment seldom even scratch the surface of what it is like being out there on your own. They can't really be expected to; the fundamental differences are enormous.

Freelancing involves surviving on your wits and talent, without a regular salary, sick pay, holiday pay or pension, without an office back-up team and without a pre-set daily routine. It requires you to specialise not diversify in terms of the service you offer, while being a generalist not a specialist in dealing with the day to day running of your business.

Freelancing may be the first time you will have put on your thinking cap and used your brains properly. If you have always felt like a square peg in a round hole, it will be the first time you will have felt at home, workwise.

Being a freelance also involves controlling the direction of your work without having the boss breathing down your neck. It means taking impulsive actions and making decisions that will alter the whole course of your life. You will have to design a new routine to suit your work. For some that means rolling out of bed at noon to start work according to their body-clock. For others it means working night and day for six months to take the rest of the year off to climb the Andes. And for a few it may mean sleeping in the car because there's no money to rent a room while you are starting up. Your only perk when times are hard like that is the knowledge that you're doing it your way.

'You have no time to make money at the start because you are too busy surviving,' says Anita Roddick. 'In the first ten or 15 years of struggling to survive you only have time to learn,' says Richard Branson.

There is a whole different structure of perks when you give up the office ones. These perks are more cerebral, and more exciting. For those of you who see a tantalising future in being a whole unto yourself, rather than a small part in a massive corporate structure, to become self-employed will probably be the most important decision you ever take.

It appears that once that leap across the great divide has been made it is hard to turn back. People who take it inevitably look on their new status with a certain awe, thrilled by their boldness and proud of their daring. There is untold self-enrichment in knowing that you're brave enough to take a challenge.

But for some, running their own business will inevitably remain a dream. Not everybody has what it takes to go out and conquer their own territory and build it into an empire. Not everybody wants to create a company of their own for the sheer thrill of doing so. You can be self-employed in a small way and still feel a success.

Before considering leaving your job (if you have one) convert into real terms the most daunting aspect of being self-employed: the prospect of living without a regular income. This, in my opinion, after talking to thousands of self-employed people, is the most salient feature of all. Would you personally be able to cope with the insecurity of irregular cash? This is what cashflow boils down to – the flowing in and out of money.

Some months when expenses are high the cash flows out far quicker than it flows in. Some months, if a job is going to take a long time to complete, the cash doesn't flow in at all. Other times you might be owed plenty of money but the client in question (usually all big companies) will only pay on statement (i.e. some time later), or find some reason not to pay at all. Not all nice people pay their bills promptly! Some months the cash doesn't flow in for the simple reason that you have not been able to find any work, or the work you have done fails to sell.

At times like this only the stark prospect of impending bankruptcy keeps you going. Inevitably, just around the corner is a flood of work. Then the question is, can you keep your head above water or are you going to be swamped by the tidal wave of commissions? Boring, self-employment is not!

Anna, a model-maker who struck out on her own after leaving art college and not finding a job, says:

> You can swing from being madly rich one month to being totally on the breadline the next. You might be paid £1,000 for a job that only took a fortnight, but then the next job might take two months during which time there will be no income. A thousand pounds doesn't go very far over two months of personal costs, business overheads and outlay on materials. You simply have to put a little stash aside to carry you over when you have a cashflow hiccup, or also find a quick, smaller job to do mid-way through to bridge the gap.

It can be chickens one day, feathers the next, as all self-employed people experience this chopping and changing of jobs at some time or another. Most of us are forced to become immune to the syndrome, otherwise we would all end up with shredded nerves. If you are an insecure type already, self-employment might not be the happy ending you are seeking . . .

Further, if you have commitments, like a family to support or a sizeable mortgage, it might be better, for the time being anyway, to stay in a salaried job. Taking risks isn't everybody's idea of fun. Shrinking from risk because of fear of failure can paralyse your enterprise. Careful planning, proper market research, effective advertising and promotion, and careful administration of your little business will make it possible to keep risks to an absolute minimum. But, to be fair, risk is something that has no hard and fast symptoms or cure. It varies with every case.

The reasons why people want to work on their own vary enormously. Different people want different things from it, put different things into it and are spurred on by reasons that range from sheer money-bent entrepreneurialism to a desperate bid for survival in the face of unrelenting unemployment. For the socially upwardly mobile, self-employment speeds up the process because you are no longer in a position where a job defines your standing. Social cross-fertilisation comes easily within the freelance society. The exception that can break the rule is the self-employed who works from home (see page 41).

Whatever the circumstances, being your own boss is going to have rewards proportional to effort and luck. The luck factor applies to everyone and luck, being the elusive thing it is, is not tangible or controllable. Being in the right place at the right time with the right contacts helps of course!

The only thing that is tangible in the early stages is your desire to start on your own. The motivation must come from you, whether it's a case of your having to work or, alternatively, needing or wanting to work. The project is inevitably fated from day one if you're forced into going freelance on the insistence of somebody else. If you don't feel you can do it, aren't sure of your single-mindedness, step back and think about it some more. You are your most important resource. In the pecking order of resources money comes third in value after you and time.

Start by examining your motivation for going solo. You are the person around whom the whole business will revolve. You don't have to be incredibly well organised or bright, but you have to have a certain amount of imagination and flair. You also have to be prepared to be logical and efficient because you must give purpose and direction to the enterprise and, after all, most of us aim for a regulated sort of life one way or another. Henceforth the buck will inevitably stop with you because you are the boss.

You are going out there to work, not play, so apply some solid self-examination. Success is within you. If you believe you can shape your destiny, you can. It is pointless to try to excuse failure with alibis like 'I never had the opportunity' or 'If only my parents had loved me'. There's no one to blame but yourself.

You have to know *why* you're going self-employed before you start.

It has often been said that man is a gregarious animal. There *are* people who enjoy being alone, but usually this is for short periods only. The idea of complete isolation is frightening to most. Individuals generally form part of a family group, part of a work circle, or part of a social gang of friends. In fact, most of our lives are based on human relationships. For the self-employed person there is always the risk that operating merrily on your own will come to be seen as slaving away in isolation. Avoid tipping that balance and you're half-way along the road to freelance success.

You also have to be prepared to undertake all the roles from boss right down to teamaker/messenger. You have to balance one managerial skill against another and you will need to wear various managerial hats. Not all of them will fit comfortably. Possibly it helps to be a bit schizophrenic! But when you have to do everything, it helps to know yourself inside-out and back-to-front before you start.

Before you can hope ever to make money you obviously have to have an idea that will work. This idea has to be tested by doing basic market research (see Chapter Four). If the idea isn't sound no amount of backing will save it from failing. Nine out of ten small businesses that fail in Britain do so because of cashflow problems (no money), usually caused by lack of planning, which boils down to lack of market research, lack of viability, lack of marketing and lack of direction. How can a bad idea badly presented hope to survive?

When you feel confident you've hit on a winner, or at least a viable project, assess your skills and how you can exploit them. Will you have to train or retrain? Will it cost time or money? Time is a most valuable resource and you have to use it well. Money can usually be raised from outside sources, not so with time.

Most people who go freelance overlook the importance of

meticulous planning. Few can afford to just wing off on a wild notion. And far too many start thinking about their new business without giving much thought to the middle-term future, a vital time which accounts for the stagnation and failure of many developing businesses. You have to be prepared to plan ahead. What is important is not where you came from but where you are going to. Work out where you want to go during, say, the next ten years. There is a formula for this called The Business Plan (see Chapter Four), which will help you plot out your direction. Even if the plan has to be adjusted from time to time it will at least give a sense of progress, something to move within and check your advancement against. John, a small City lunch-time caterer, comments:

My biggest oversight in the early days was underestimating how successful my business was to become. The wheels had for some time turned smoothly and the cogs had all slipped neatly into place for a modestly small business. But I hadn't made any provision for expansion. I should have thought about that before I baked my first pie instead of spending five years running round in circles trying to tie the unplanned bits together.

Making an initial outline plan in which to operate is essential. After all, from Day One you are in charge. You are no longer an employee. People are going to pay you for being a specialist at the job they want you to do for them.

Sometimes you will work unguided on your own for your clients (no longer your bosses!) and sometimes you will be expected to join the work-force in their offices as a complement to the team. Nobody there is going to help you define your own personal working outline. You will have to devise a lifestyle that allows you to work to your own rules and allows you the freedom to enjoy it.

Unless you join a co-operative or form a partnership you are going to find yourself alone when it comes to thinking your business out. It might need start-up capital if you have to purchase equipment and stock, rent premises or hire labour. You might have savings to get along with, but if you don't you will have to sit down and systematically do a survey covering your present assets and projected financial requirements.

Nowadays banks and other sources of funds are *reasonably* well-versed in loans for small businesses and are tolerant towards their ups and downs (see Chapter Eight). Bank managers, in spite of

Mark Twain's observation about them being people who 'lend you an umbrella when the sun shines but want it back when it begins to rain', are there to promote a healthy financial economy. Providing start-up funds for a business that is to thrive can only make more funds, if not for the bank at least for the economy.

It's impossible to quantify exactly what being a freelance is going to involve but the preceeding few pages will have given you an idea of what you can expect to cope with for starters.

It's not hard to find help and guidance on all the aspects covered (see Contacts, Networks, Reading and your local reference library). Chapter Three expands on the aspects they never tell you about, like the more cerebral side of working in isolation and keeping the mind fired up and confidence blooming through high points and low. I have always found the freelance community to be a closely-knit and supportive one. While there is still healthy competition within the ranks, off-duty we all speak the same language and understand the basic freelance truths that operate on a universal level, things like the pride of real achievement in the face of almost insurmountable odds on the sometimes long climb to the top.

Who freelancing is for

So who are the people who are most likely to want to take the freelance alternative?

There have always been self-employed people. Some people become self-employed because their job was going nowhere. Some used it as a stepping stone between being an employee and becoming an employer running a small business. Others, like writers, artists and craftsmen, have traditionally been self-employed. But now the freelance alternative is being picked up by just about everybody who wants a change. It goes without saying that aspiring entrepreneurs will latch on to it. And the powers that be hope it will prove to be the missing ingredient for renewed British greatness.

Statistics show that the self-employed are usually middle-aged and married, a catchment area that includes the new, growing corps of freelancers, those over 40 who have been made redundant.

The Labour Force Survey lists almost half of the self-employed as being in the 30 to 44 age range. There are good reasons for this, notably that the skills, experience and confidence required for running your own single-person business or small company can usually only be gleaned after some years in the labour force.

ENTREPRENEURS

In the United States the entrepreneur is often defined as one who starts his or her own, new and small business. Equally, it could be somebody who creates a new market and a new customer.

Innovation is the specific tool of entrepreneurs, the means by which they exploit change as an opportunity for a different business or a different service. The practice of innovation is not something that comes automatically. It can, to a degree, be learnt. Planning, as the term is commonly understood, is actually incompatible with an entrepreneurial society, character and economy. Consequently, while many of us would like to think of ourselves as entrepreneurs, few of us possess the talent to spot an opportunity or have the split-second timing and nerves of steel needed to take advantage of it.

Luck is important, too, and some people are definitely lucky. It's something you are born with. You may not think you have it, but I maintain that it is something you can nurture with a positive attitude and enthusiasm. Life is much easier when luck plays *with* you rather than *against*. Field Marshal Montgomery always used to question potential officers to find out if they were lucky people. I don't know if his lucky officers were less likely to be shot than the unlucky ones, but there may have been something in his approach that helped foster feelings of being lucky in his men. (It goes without saying, of course, that just being lucky is not going to be enough when you are trying to move your idea forward one step at a time. But it certainly helps!)

FORMER OFFICE TYPES

The true entrepreneur represents only the thinnest slice of the freelance cake. Up there alongside them, or perhaps slightly lower down the success scale, will be all those bored, fired or redundant executives being hired in a 'Rent-A-Boss' capacity or acting as freelance consultants. There are also a large proportion of the 'baby boomers' (the Sixties people, ex-hippies, drop-outs from way back, the non-conformists) who will probably continue to choose the freelance option. So will the smart young employees who tire of being kept down by a plodding corporate society in which each waits in line for promotion on the basis of time-serving rather than on merit.

Josie, once a PA in an engineering company, now a private home computer teacher, recalls:

> *I was just so fed up of being passed over for an increase in both salary and status that I chucked it in. The man I was working for was genuinely dumb and made sure I didn't overshadow him. I was ready to eclipse him!*

It has always been simple, by the nature of their work, for consultants of any kind (see Chapter Eleven) to prefer the freelance option. These people are usually former staffers who have broken away to concentrate on their own speciality under their own banner.

TRADITIONAL FREELANCE ACTIVITIES

People in the arts always have been freelance. Actors, singers and dancers, unless contracted to a company, are lone rangers. So are many writers, photographers, designers, stylists, editors, sportsmen, counsellors, therapists, models, translators, artists and craftspeople.

In the freelance service economy there are a growing number of people doing jobs relating to computers, marketing, PR, research, information, market research and business services. Many caterers, cleaners, farm workers and maintenance people also operate as freelancers.

THE YOUNGER GENERATION

Self-employment is still rare among younger workers. The Labour Force Survey reveals that only 1·6 per cent of all self-employed workers are under 19 years old. Changing work patterns do not promise a lot for unskilled school-leavers.

Jobs are already hard to find and hard to keep. And even with the help of the various Youth Training Schemes they often boil down to nothing more than cheap labour. Some young people may never find work. The 16 to 18-year-olds are the first to be taken out of the labour market. Consequently it's going to take an extremely determined and streetwise spirit to go solo so young. The twilight zone of neither here nor there with no boss or fellow workers, can prove impossible for somebody with no work structure to depend on.

However, I have met several teenagers who have started off with small-scale, fairly menial businesses like washing cars and windows, babysitting, house-watching, doing manual chores and other unskilled activities which people are prepared to pay for. Their futures as freelancers are by no means guaranteed, but at least, with an experience of earning, their inclination to try working outside the system has been stimulated. Billy, now 20 and owner of a registered landscaping supplies company, remembers:

> When my father was made unemployed and I left school with no chance of anything half-way decent to do, I got so depressed sitting at home watching the box that I went round the houses knocking on doors and asking for gardening work. Of course I picked on rich areas with big gardens. They were all so desperate for somebody to help them that eventually I employed my father to help me!

THE RETIRED

At the other end of the scale are the pensioners. In Britain there are 10 million people over retirement age, who make up more than 17 per cent of the population. Eleven per cent of the self-employed are pensioners.

After a lifetime of organised work people facing retirement can be overjoyed at the prospect of years of freedom ahead on a pension. But equally they can become deeply depressed. Work can be a joy in itself. Idleness can be hell. According to Age Concern, 75 per cent of elderly people are healthy enough to live normal lives and carry out normal duties without help. The majority of voluntary work is done by people aged 65 to 74. Increasingly, with people being offered or asked to take early retirement at 50 and 55, pensioners are retrenching, using their past business experience.

The law currently allows pensioners to earn a set amount (£75 a week in 1987) without losing their state pensions. With a lifetime's accumulated wisdom and experience to draw on, carrying on frequently comes more easily than accepting inactivity and endless leisure time. Hugh, a pensioner, says:

> *I was lucky when I left the Civil Service to turn my hobby, restoring custom cars, into a proper business. I knew for one thing that I could probably make more money from it than I was earning as a civil servant, if I approached it properly. Retirement would have come as a very bitter ending to a lifetime of work if I'd had nothing to dive into.*

REDUNDANTS

Made unemployed, through staff cutbacks, through closures of factories, mines, mills and the introduction of newly-automated operations, the future for many is the dole queue – and (usually) an immediate change in lifestyle.

Bitter and angry at being rejected and (nowadays) considered too old for many of the jobs on offer, the most common reaction of those who have been made redundant (for 'redundant' read 'fired') is to want never to be in a position where anybody could fire them again.

Explains one redundant executive:

> *At the moment of being fired an individual feels out of control. And, in fact, at that time they are out of control of their careers. They very quickly realise they have to find other real options. In reality there are numerous other options, the most likely being to try self-employment. There is no chance of you firing yourself!*

The redundant worker with a lump sum in his pocket will be in a marginally better frame of mind than the unemployed one who suddenly finds himself out of work with nothing.

THE UNEMPLOYED

Looking behind the headlines on the state of affairs in the world of unemployment we find only a moderately thriving community of the formerly unemployed running businesses of their own. As unemployment becomes a permanent fact of life, the numbers of hard-core self-employed workers will undoubtably increase as the unemployed look for alternatives to life on the dole.

However, setting up a business in depressed areas like Newcastle and Liverpool, where an awful lot of people are unemployed and don't have the money to pay somebody else to do for them that which they could do themselves, is no easy task. The knock-on effect of one major closure can reach right through a community to local service industries and can suffocate a good freelance idea before it ever gets off the ground. Alan, a former coalminer, comments:

> *There was nothing I could see myself doing. I went on a couple of adult education courses on Starting in Business and eventually formed a small co-op with some mates repairing farming equipment. For three years we didn't declare it because we had to use our social security to survive on. No bank would loan us a penny as we had no security. Now we can just tick over. At least we have our self respect not having to queue up for our hand-outs every week.*

THE DISABLED

Another group that finds self-employment a satisfactory means of earning a living are the disabled, who may rarely make contact with the outside world. Julie, a polio victim who works from a wheelchair, says:

> *I put an ad in the local paper offering book-keeping services and now I have three clients who bring their books to me every week. I don't earn a fortune but it's the highlight of my week getting visited by my clients.*

HOME-BASED MOTHERS

Many self-employed people choose to work from home (it's cheaper than renting an office and family life need not suffer), and there is a substantial home-based freelance population in the form of mothers who are bringing up children while working (often profitably). Many of them may have put off childbearing in order to get established in their jobs, but were not encouraged to return to work after they had their babies.

Naturally, this cuts both ways. The firm that trains a woman at enormous cost only to find that a year later she wants to have time off to start a family, frequently resents this as it finds that women who are out of the mainstream for a period of time lose momentum and fail to keep up with current developments in their field.

Margaret, a salesperson for a large photographic studio, says:

My boss was terribly keen to have me back, but when the time came management had brought in a younger man, trained him comprehensively and I had been conveniently phased out.

Women have the right to return to work up to 29 weeks after birth, but they may not have the right if they work for a small firm with five or less employees. However, employers are allowed to offer suitable alternative work rather than give back the old job.

Those who do return tend to find that they have fallen way behind their contemporaries and are unlikely to make up for lost time. It is difficult enough to move up the organisational hierarchy in old-guard companies where there is still discrimination against women workers. (A survey done in 1987 by a large management consultancy showed that one-third of senior [male] managers felt that women were unsuitable for management work.) Some women returners lose heart and drift away into part-time work of an untaxing nature (like typing/shop attending). Others become flexi-mums, working as part-time mothers and part-time workers, either sharing a job with another or splitting it by dividing it in two separate activities.

Female self-employment has grown enormously over the past decade. Women, given the chance, are excellent when it comes to rustling up work and perfectly able to run a straightforward business, having had the experience of running the family, house and housekeeping accounts in the past. Also a woman's approach to budgeting tends to be more realistic than that of men, who are often used only to the big company budget style of fiscal planning. Kate, a translator, is supporting her three childen while her husband retrains:

I've always budgeted my life with military-style discipline. Earning a limited amount and having only limited time I work my budget round both money and time. Time, which I now think of as money, I've always divided into categories: children's time, family time, my time. The same with available money. If you can run a family you can run a business.

The developing world of computers has swollen the outworker pitch with mainly women operators, many with small children, who are encouraged by big companies to plug into their terminals at home.

Maggy Meade-King, the *Guardian* journalist who writes their excellent 'Workface' section, comments:

I'm not at all convinced that this is the wonderful answer for home-based women that it is supposed to be. These new initiatives to make things better can end up with a lot of home-based people trapped in part-time work doing the same tedious job, like computer work, but from separate little boxes instead of with others in an office environment. It's socially lonely and you tend to be unaware of what's going on outside your front door. Support groups like the Working Mothers' Association are essential. Neighbourhood network stations are being built up, with homeworkers working together and sharing facilities, to avoid these problems. I don't think working from home should be made to sound easy. It is not easy making a profit while breastfeeding, and it is very difficult to get something off the ground when there are three pre-school babies in tow. Working at home for women means having two jobs because, unlike the spouse who has his wife to back him up, she has nobody there to help with either the domestic work or her money-making endeavours.

3

THE FREELANCE
MENTALITY

The self-employed state of mind is fascinatingly unpredictable. I would list discipline, determination, drive and daring as constant and essental characteristics, plus a dash of cunning and loads of common sense. Leaving the safety of the system to take on all the toil, worry and uncertainty of working for yourself has to indicate that you prefer to walk on the wild side – and have the resilience to bounce back.

You definitely have to have guts – and a sense of humour – to set up on your own. When I say that in the introduction class of a Starting In Business course I teach at London's City University, I usually see about a third of the assembled students shrink visibly. I know that by about Class Four they will have left to join Bookbinding, Basket-weaving or French, or some other class that is not going to force them to put their necks on the line. To be a half-way effective freelancer you have to be prepared to put a lot of neck on the line.

The fierce independent spirit that is unwilling to tolerate less than you perceive yourself capable of will be a driving force. It will either drive you round the bend with frustration or it will drive you to the top. The true measure of the independent spirit lies in the desire to succeed on your own terms, and in order to do that you have to have nerves of steel. This ethos can be developed and heightened, but if you don't have it in your make-up it is questionable whether or not you will acquire it *en route*.

The top in the case of the self-employed worker is not a fixed point. For some it is enough cash to survive on and the rewards of doing painstakingly superb work. For others it is making a packet and being famous. Some start up because they need to do something for themselves. Others just want to maintain a comfortable self-employed level and do only as much work as is needed to spend those cold winters in the sunny south, painting, diving, restoring a barn or whatever it is that there was never time enough to indulge in before.

I can already hear some readers muttering 'nonsense' and 'pipe dreams'! It is well-known that the self-employed do *not* stop working or say 'no' when there's enough work or money to get along with. 'You always think it's the last time the phone will ring,' Les Dawson says.

By the time that stage is reached the ambitious soul has been so honed to achievement that it becomes psychologically impossible to say 'no' to more work and one ends up by taking on bigger, better and braver projects on top of an already full schedule!

However, the choice, difficult as it is, will always be yours and yours alone. Make the right choice and you might soar to formerly unexperienced heights; make the wrong one and it's purgatory. Make a sensible, cautious choice and your conscience will niggle away at you, suggesting that you could have been more ambitious. Make one mad promise in the heat of the moment and you might get eaten up by anxiety for weeks.

It's often a no-win situation, but if you have a questioning mind, active sense of exploration and a zest for living life to the full then self-employment is the only route.

Even in my darkest moments when there had been no work, the cashflow was flowing in the wrong direction, and I had killer flu (knowing that every day spent in bed had earned exactly £0.00), not for one moment did I consider the option of returning to regular employment. I have now developed a health tolerance that only collapses on bank holidays!

The extent to which the self-employed have a deep disregard for corporate life cannot be overstated enough. Once solo, always solo. A freelance could never accept being part of a large, protective organisation again. If you learn to tolerate the lifestyle it's a much, much sounder way to live.

The first analysis

The arguments for and against working for yourself are familiar territory. Lists like the following appear in virtually every handout promoting self-employment from banks to outlets like the Small Firms Service. It is important to at least read them, as they are a valuable rule of thumb guide for those who think they would be happy on their own.

They can be summed up as follows.

For:
1 I would like to be my own boss.
2 I would like to work at something that interests me.
3 I would like to be independent and make my own considered decisions.
4 I would like to organise my work schedule and time myself.
5 I would like to build up my self-confidence and ego.
6 I would like to learn about business and how to run one.
7 I would like to present myself and my business efficiently and with style to the outside world.
8 I would like to be able to use money creatively.
9 I would like to plan my next ten years as a solo worker.
10 I would like to think up and research a marketable idea.

Tick each one honestly. In this test clearly the idea is to score ten out of ten, but aim for the reality not the fantasy.

If you score eight to ten ticks you are the type to be attracted by the idea of working on your own account. If the score is five to eight you are certainly drawn to the idea but should find out more about it. Less than five suggests you should not really be considering self-employment. Many people are not of the right temperament to set up on their own.

Against:
By being self-employed you will probably have to:
1 Work a lot on your own, often at nights and weekends, despite beckoning diversions such as the pub, television or the family.
2 Spend all your savings and probably have to borrow from the bank or other sources.
3 Find somewhere to work either at home or in an office.
4 Take a course to train in new skills or refresh old ones.

5 Never have a regular salary or a pension, other than the State or a privately-funded one.
6 Hustle work convincingly, often to or from strangers.
7 Listen to strong criticism and challenging advice.
8 Cope under stress and never let things drift.
9 Make all the decisions.
10 Do everything, from messenger to manager.

If the above ten options seem good news to you, you should have been on your own years ago. If they appear tedious and too much like hard work, change your attitude or stay in the job you're in.

Too many people make the mistake of thinking that once they're in charge of their own show it's going to be glory all the way. The glory only comes when you've pushed and shoved yourself to self-start. Like an old car, human batteries go flat quite often!

To start with, few people will give a damn either way whether you're doing your own thing or not. They find it terminally dull, particularly if they are still in employment, when you complain about having failed to make any money (let alone a profit) for two or three months. Cast your memory back to when you had a job yourself.

Other freelancers in the same position might be sympathetic, but if they are walking that self-employed tightrope of few returns until business is established, they might find it too close to home for comfort.

Fully employed people seldom understand what being freelance is really like. They belong to a body of workers sheltered by the corporation umbrella. You must make do with just your tiny hand-held brolly for protection. When things go wrong in the office it might not be too serious and anyway the blame can be shared around, losses easily absorbed. When they go wrong for an independent, it can be catastrophic.

As an independent, every time you take a day off sick or go on a course or go to buy some piece of equipment nobody pays you for the time this takes. When you take a week or a month off to go on holiday there will be a visible gap in your earnings. Every time you pick up your telephone or write a letter you know that you will have to pay for it out of your own funds. For the office worker these are accepted perks along with photocopying machines, equipment, subsidised canteens, the company car, the clothes allowance, private health scheme, and so on.

But then no regular staffer will ever be able to take six weeks off to sail round the Med or six months off to climb the Himalayas without losing their job (unless they are on a sabbatical). No regular staffer will be able to control the direction in which their jobs are going without the boss having the final say. Nor will they be able to roll out of bed at midday, pull on a tracksuit and start work at lunchtime if they had had a heavy night.

The Psychology

Occasionally a news item will mention the increasing numbers of the self-employed. Quite often a government bulletin will stress that the need to understand and foster self-employment is being solved by more enterprise agencies. From time to time a feature crops up in a magazine about working from home and how jolly it is, making millions while the children sleep peacefully in the next room. (Sometimes it *is* like that, but the actual picture might be of the harassed mother or father trying to keep the children's jammy fingerprints off the typing/graphics/pistons/architectural drawings they are working on on the kitchen table while placating the bawling baby in the corner!)

Generally not a lot is said about the inner side of freelancing, the emotional side. The psychology of the self-employed person has not yet been fully explored and there is precious little written about it. Far more column inches have been dedicated to the psychology of the unemployed than to that of the self-employed.

Whether working for yourself at home, alone or surrounded by family, or in an office, shared or solo, freelancing comes with a fairly exclusive set of ticklish psychological problems that you should at least be aware of. Knowing about them won't necessarily mean that you can prevent them, but at least they won't pounce so devastatingly when you least expect them.

Self-discipline

Let's start with self-discipline. This concerns all freelance souls, but particularly those working from home, an option many freelancers choose when they're getting going and don't yet want to commit themselves to renting an office. Home-based work is the area that requires the most rigid self-discipline, if only to keep Monday Malady at bay. (Monday Malady, or Mondayish, is defined in Webster's *New International Dictionary* as 'Characteristic of Monday, fagged out after Sunday'. Normally, self-employed people don't suffer the Monday Malady as often as their employed counterparts as they have the option of working Sunday and sleeping in on Monday!)

As I sit writing this on my Amstrad, the sun pouring in through my windows, gentle Mozart on the tape, a beautiful vase of flowers on the desk in front of me, cup of freshly roasted coffee in my hand and the cats snuggled up at my feet, the advantages of working from home are clear. I've read my mail over breakfast, sitting in the morning's tranquillity on the verandah, and caught up with world news over a second cup of coffee. Because my routine decrees that I only start work at 10 a.m. I didn't bother to get up until about 9.15.

Oh, sigh my few employed friends, you're so *lucky*. You work from home. You don't have to get up early to catch a bus or a train to work and then sit through a day of chaos and chatter, taking orders from a boss who is inevitably in a bad mood.

Absolutely true. I remember the office routine as being complete hell.

Instead I now saunter around in comfortable clothes, never having to panic about being late, always proceeding in a relaxed manner to my study ready to dive into work. On good days it's bliss. It's the sort of paradise I dreamt of when I was cooped up in a noisy newsroom where the clatter of typewriters meant you couldn't hear yourself think.

But come the bad days . . . While I know there are no bad days, just bad attitudes about days, I'd still give my eyeteeth for the faithful, trusty team of colleagues who would be there to stop me staring silently at the keyboard. I often wonder, on those days, if anybody (other than the bank manager) would ever notice if I never wrote another word.

On bad days being home-based boils down to fighting off apathy and lack of motivation and forcing yourself out of bed. Having no threat – like an angry boss shouting at you because you're late – hanging over your head can wear down the backbone of any self-starter.

Getting out of bed can be a killer. Lying there, thinking about the millions of things you have to do, what order to do them in, how to do them, etc., etc. can put you off the day entirely. It is not every day that you are going to work at things you love. There will always be a certain amount of dreary drudgery whether you are employed or self-employed.

If you live alone you run the risk of staying in bed indefinitely, though if you have to make dozens of telephone calls it can be a pleasant little diversion from the usual routine to make them from bed. Nobody will know you're still there as you merrily negotiate new contracts from under the duvet. Equally, they won't know either that you're struggling with terminal lethargy. One or two words of encouragement or nagging from someone else would be of enormous help at a time like this. It is quite disabling and extraordinary how weak the flesh is when the spirit is off-key.

Having finally managed to prise yourself out of bed, dragging on that boring old pair of jeans instead of nice going-to-town clothes can depress you even further. The debate about whether to shave/wash your hair/put on make-up or not is given up because you know nobody's going to see you anyway.

Looking and feeling frightful, you stagger to your workplace and sit down unhappily to work in solitary confinement waiting for somebody to ring. And we all know that on *those* days the phone never rings.

Left alone to master the fragile psychology of survival in isolation you learn quite a few home truths about yourself. Not all of them are pleasant but many of them turn into confidence-boosters as you build your ego up and watch yourself turn into one of life's survivors. Take strength in the knowledge that there are very, very few people who are natural self-starters. To get yourself going in the morning and keep yourself working with a certain momentum is tough, especially when you know there is nobody there to catch you skiving. (See Chapter 6 for routines.)

It is, naturally, very different for a freelancer with children, where the equivalent of the nine-to-five routine and rush hour is replaced by the domestic routine of seeing spouses off to work and sorting out the kids. The home-based work schedule will have to be worked round the family timetable and might end up as a few hours in the morning and a few hours after dinner.

But either way, the strictest self-discipline has to apply. Domestic distractions are notorious. Ask any self-employed homebaser what the hardest aspect is and I guarantee you it will be the Distraction Factor: the irresistible distraction of making another cup of coffee/ mending the car/hoovering/spraying the roses/clearing out the hall cupboard, etc. It is a genuine dilemma to find the right balance between endless procrastination and workaholism – the other end of the scale. When your work has no set start or end there is always something else you could be doing. David, formerly an English teacher, now a copywriter, comments:

> *It is very easy to find at least two dozen things I must do in the house before I sit down at my desk.*
>
> *To get started in the morning I have to set the alarm, get instantly out of bed, switch on the radio and be active workwise within 60 minutes otherwise my whole day disappears. Luckily I have two noisy, hungry cats to remind me to wake up! I keep intending to go jogging but I find my race against the clock in the mornings sets me up quite well!*

After the first flush of independence you will probably have to start tricking yourself into starting the daily ball rolling. Stick to whatever form of self-monitoring suits you, but expect to have to alter it from time to time. If you are shrewd enough to set up in business you are shrewd enough to get out of being cornered by your own self-monitoring devices.

It can help to set a deadline. If you're not at your desk or workbench or telephone by a set time then punish yourself in some way. If you make the deadline before time give yourself credit. Reward yourself for good work and good time kept. Buy yourself flowers, good wine and chocolates. Take an afternoon off to go to a matinee. Go to town to meet a friend for lunch. If you do what should have taken you five days in four, take the fifth day off and enjoy yourself. Nobody else is going to give you a day off so make sure you look after yourself. A little spoiling keeps the negatives at bay!

Lis, a mother of two, who, after being inspired by a working-from-home book, now indexes books from home, describes it:

> *Every second of my day is planned. I have to watch the clock and pace myself and play by my own rules. I do only house vitals and make sure I take all of Sunday off, however much work there is.*
>
> *Time has a completely different slant for me now and I control it the way that suits me best. For example, I make sure I keep my regular lunch-dates with friends. And even if I'm under enormous pressure I take time off for something like a run to loosen me up. As soon as I start to feel all tense and my shoulders rise up to my ears, I know my self-esteem is on the way down and I have to get up and recharge.*

Self-esteem

Self-esteem is something, like self-discipline, that must be kept in good order. Self-esteem is believing you can do the job. There's nobody around to tell you you can, so you have to keep telling yourself. It is too easy to persuade yourself that you can't do something or that it isn't worth doing. With that attitude your little business would very soon be on the rocks.

To many outsiders, working from home is not doing a 'real' job. Consequently in their eyes you are less valid and can lack status. This can actually be worse for men who work from home and are sometimes taken to be hopeless wets because they don't go out to earn a living. Women have an easier deal here, thanks to long-standing custom and thought. Liz, a caner who started caning and rushing after reading a library book on the subject when looking for way to top up the family budget, explains:

> *I found myself making a point of continuing working if friends dropped in for tea, letting them see me work.*
>
> *Pretty soon they saw I was serious about it. They end up taking you seriously and become quite intrigued, and, I think, rather envious.*

You have to be firm with friends who drop by, telling them that you can only spend half an hour over a quick cup of coffee with them. It might not be in your nature to be anti-social. But if you're a freelance it should be in your nature to survive, which makes saying 'no' an essential part of your make-up. It can be interesting to observe yourself putting your foot down in situations where previously you might have bent over backwards in an effort to please.

Self-watching

It makes interesting self-watching to see how people tend to lean less on you when they find you're being firm about issues like wasting time, and how once you get over feeling guilty about not pleasing everyone you perceive yourself as a much more rounded, self-possessed individual.

As your business grows and you grow with it, whether home- or office-based, the likelihood of seeing friends and having a normal social life becomes more and more remote. Even if you employ people and delegate or out-source you can easily find yourself being totally absorbed, fascinated and excited by developments.

It is not impossible that you will find yourself working on something that interests you so passionately that it becomes far more diverting and entertaining than meeting chums for a natter or organising a dinner party. While you are only interested in your newfound passion, others will perceive you differently.

People tend to call an absorption with work workaholism but in many cases it's not. It's just a matter of the work in hand being more riveting than the gang. And more profitable! I often find myself constructing elaborate excuses for not socialising because I'm enjoying some piece of work.

According to the monthly *Management Psychology*, the best way to say 'no' gracefully to an invitation without hurting the person's feelings is the 'I'd love to, but unfortunately I'm working on a report that must be in the mail by three' approach. For years I tried this but inevitably became caught in my own web of white lies. Which report? When?

But then a friend told me the easiest way: have a sign attached to the telephone saying, 'I'm terribly sorry, that's impossible.' Very few people are going to ask why and nobody will check up later because they never knew what it was you were standing them up for.

If doing this makes you feel bad, try to see it in terms of time management. Joan, owner of a secretarial and conference agency she formed when her marriage broke up, says:

It really depends on what you want from your life. If you concentrate your energies on your special goals – success, profit, reputation, achievement – you can easily become cut off from human contact, both mentally and socially. That's okay if you're aware of it, but you should make an effort to keep yourself in circulation, seeing friends and colleagues, hearing what's going on and being on the circuit to find out who's moved where.

It is far easier to find work through an old associate (who might have been promoted) than it is to find work from a stranger who probably has his or her own posse of freelancers already. It's the old 'who you know' routine that frequently gets the work.

When Barry Norman was made redundant in 1971 after 12 years on a national newspaper he spent some of the redundancy money on smart new clothes.

Then I went and sat in a Fleet Street bar with a bottle of champagne and chatted to my old friends. It was my form of psychological warfare.

Soon various editors started to sidle up to me, assuming that because I looked so spruce I was doing very well. They'd say 'Listen old boy, I imagine you must be very busy but I wonder if you could fit in a couple of days' feature writing for me?' And slowly but surely work started coming in.

Although a book shouldn't be judged by its cover, it often is. If you're the book make sure the cover looks good. If you're offering an office or business service dress like a smart executive. If you're working in the media, arts or design try to dress with the flair that suits the occasion.

It will give you confidence. It's worth making the effort because you no longer belong anywhere; you are an outsider and therefore difficult to pigeon-hole. You no longer have the automatic power you used to have to influence the organisations you work for. You don't hear what's going on on the office grapevine so you no longer know the short-cuts and codewords. People will only feel confident about letting you into their in-house secrets and sub-plots if you seem to be one of them.

It is an interesting predicament. On one hand, as an independent you have much going for you, on the other, there is a degree of powerlessness. This predicament breeds self-doubt, the fastest downer of all, so beware. There is no known way to immunise yourself against failure or feelings of failure and you might not get much sympathy from your employed acquaintances.

I used to attempt to explain the nuts and bolts of going solo but soon gave up. My colleagues on site would knock off at the five o'clock whistle and then ride me for not coming to the pub with them. I started by explaining I needed to get back to my tele-phone before six to organise more work or buy supplies before the building merchants closed. They just thought I'd turned very dull. They made me feel very isolated at first but I don't care now. Ray, carpenter.

Isolation

It's not surprising that the self-employed tend to stick together. With little moral support around, due mainly to the lack of under-standing of the freelance alternative, support networks are growing up. These link lines are of a professional nature, and more personal now that people are admitting that they find being self-employed a lonely business, particularly if they work at home.

Without creating formal groups, the freelance community seems to be gravitating towards fellow souls. Often two or three from similar professions split an office, for economic reasons and for the company and sounding-board that others provide. 'In the time spent chatting with somebody else I fire away and spark like mad, but with no imput I produce nothing new', says Bill, a graphic designer.

Psychologically, if you find your own company uninspiring it can be a lifesaver to have somebody else there. Better still if you can bounce ideas off each other and use the same resources. Even to have somebody to go to the pub with at lunchtime and share problems or ideas with helps! No man is an island. Loneliness affects everybody at some time. It's important to ensure that you're not always going to be surrounded by things that you have to do on your own, and attempt to organise your business and social schedules in a way that will force you to leave the house or office at some time of the day.

But perhaps the most important part of linking up is when things go well and there is somebody there to give you a pat on the back.

Business Opportunity Digest, the publication of the Institute of Small Business, an organisation started 11 years ago to help people get into business, works as a mouthpiece for people on their own and features success stories, ideas, views and news from the world's business press. Editor Conor MacGillycuddy comments:

> *The results are always hard to interpret. We run lots of success stories, especially the ones along the 'I thought it was all over' line written by a redundant 47-year-old with a heart complaint who now has a turnover of a million. It's big relief for others out there who are unsure of themselves. It serves as succour during those bleak times. Many people are having good results but have nobody around to tell them so. Quite often they are unaware of it altogether until they read something about somebody in a similar situation.*

While *BOD* is aimed at small business people doing their own thing at a reasonably high level of operation, there is another publication called *Homebase* which is geared to the person who works from home and, like *BOD*, is absolutely packed with triumphs and traumas. When Chris Oliver, an ex-social-worker who has spent 15 years working at home because of illness, launched this freelancers' newsletter the result was quite overwhelming. Hundreds of lonely freelancers wrote in to share their experiences and say what they felt to other people who cared. Chris comments:

Most of them say the same thing. They feel they are the only people living that way. It's a creeping isolation, even for those who like working by themselves. I don't really know anybody who is doing the same as I am. People outside the system need to know what other people in their field are doing. I hope Homebase serves as a bit of a lifeline for those floundering in the deep water before they get to their dream island.

Toughening up

The multiple nature of the freelancer can be confusing. One minute you're going for business in a hard-hitting way, the next doing the books or typing letters and invoices. A bit later you're out delivering the goods.

Emil started his own PR business after working for various agencies:

I work from my flat but never let on how small my business – which is booming – is. It's far better to let the clients think I'm much more corporate than I am. I always talk in the corporate 'we'. If somebody rings to check an account I will say 'our' accountant will see to it. Of course, it is I who scuttles off to sort it out!

I've learnt certain little telephone tricks, like suggesting I have a second line! They're spending good money and want to believe I have rows and rows of minions in th background, so I don't suggest for a moment that I don't have! On the few occasions I have in help I make sure that they answer the phone, my only aural image yardstick, in a terrifically smart way. It's important they create the right image. I ask them to say things like, 'He's away from his desk' or 'He's with a client' if I'm out, which sounds like I'm a going concern. There is nothing more infuriating for an important caller than to get some officious aide who sounds like they're chewing gum and drinking tea while answering the phone.

Presentation of the right image is all part of the self-employed package and has to be done effectively, otherwise you are just wasting your time, energy and, ultimately, money. (See Chapter 5).

So much of being self-employed is common sense. This is probably why a large proportion of the populace are unsuited to this sort of life! But combined with common sense must be awareness. According to Harry Levinson, in his book *The Exceptional Executive*, the major difference between the successful and unsuccessful business person is awareness.

Family pressures

Self-employment is more complex if you run a family and business under the same roof. It's homebody versus breadwinner and you have to be prepared for a whole new set of feelings. This can especially be true of the relationship where your partner does a boring 9-to-5 job under the eye of a dreadful boss and can't wait to get home and relax, only to find you working ebulliently, empire-building every available minute.

Unless you have total understanding and back-up from your family there may be resentment from their side if they feel that you (mother/father or offspring) are overlooking them in favour of personal gain and ego-tripping, and an undercurrent of guilt on your side if you feel this might be true, even if you are working to support them. Family loyalties are touchy things. Even though a lot of spouses help run their partner's business, an 'abandoned' spouse who feels he or she has been overshadowed by your business is an extremely unhappy one. The same applies to children and parents who suddenly find you don't have half the time for them you used to.

Every time the phone rings out of business hours and interferes with family life, you want to rip the plug out at the wall. Conversely, when it rings during work hours and the kids are brawling in the background, you want to rip your hair out (or theirs) as your carefully created business image goes up the spout.

The question you should have asked yourself is: Can I handle a wide variety of roles? It's difficult enough being the boss as well as the book-keeper, secretary, teamaker, hustler, labourer, brilliant innovator and the bod who sells. Wearing the half-homebody, half-entrepreneur trilby as well is even more confusing. Unless you clear this up immediately it will undoubtably get worse as your business grows.

It is easy to lose sight of priorities when the pace heats up. Tension runs high and soon you're confronted with burn-out from mis-managed expansion instead of the expected elation from success.

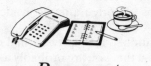

Burn-out

Sod's Law dictates that when you've actually decided to take time off, the phone will never stop ringing with offers of work. When you are already overloaded with work, more and more well-paid assignments will come hurtling towards you, begging to be done. You don't want to say 'no' because: (a) the client might shrug and strike you off their list of available outsiders because you're obviously too busy, (b) the extra money will come in useful when you get round to taking a holiday/building the back extension/buying a new car; (c) to have your work placed in that particular outlet would be good for your reputation.

You say 'yes', put it in the already bulging Work Commissioned file and settle down to burn more midnight oil. Everybody can burn the candle at both ends. Most of us enjoy doing it sometimes. All self-employed people seem to do it without a second thought, even those right at the top of the tree, which makes them more at risk from the dreaded burn-out.

The late Liberace, for example, while doing his show at Las Vegas was also recording his own television special. The result was a total collapse and some weeks spent resting. His comment: 'I guess I've been burning the candelabra at both ends.' The long and the short of it is that he lost two months' income while recovering.

When the red light flashes 'burn-out', heed its message. You have reached exhaustion point. Stop and take a rest. You can't do everything for everybody all the time.

Burn-out is a very specific thing and you have to learn to avoid it, otherwise it will strike at some time or another. It's not something reserved for the ranks of the self-employed, but by dint of being self-employed one sails closer to the wind.

The causes of burn-out are exhaustion, worry, insecurity and all the things that go with them, like not enough money, not enough time, not enough inclination, too much work, too much drink, too much responsibility, too much coffee. (An ingredient in coffee – and tea – called chloregenic acid destroys thiamine (Vitamin B_1), a nutrient essential to the health of the nervous system. If you drink more than three cups of coffee a day consider taking B-complex tablets to be safe.)

All the above-mentioned are fairly normal day-to-day anxieties exacerbated by the fact that you are probably a creative and capable individual and, because of that, may suffer mid-life crisis, when it comes, more severely than those with less responsibility.

Executive stress in large corporations is now costing British firms between £3.5 billion and £10.5 billion a year, according to estimates from the stress specialist consultancy Health and Safety Services. A university study found that it cost between one and three per cent of Britain's Gross National Product.

Stress is worse for the self-employed because there is no secure framework in their lives. There is no regular pattern or office back-up system available to cushion you while you work your way through your problems.

Nobody will pay you do take a few days off to catch up. No colleague can cover for you so you can slow down and take it easy. Usually you just have to soldier on. Everything non-essential has to fall by the wayside. With a minimum of expenditure of energy and spirit you continue to cope with the project(s) in hand until you see the light at the end of the tunnel. It would be far too costly to your reputation, quite apart from your bank balance, to let things get out of hand.

Ruth, an actress specialising in one-woman shows, explains her approach:

I put myself on auto-pilot for non-essentials when this happens and I'm in the middle of travelling the country with a couple of different shows. I can't allow myself to be deflected by domestic matters. It is very selfish, but it is me or bust otherwise. Eventually I'll get round to having a physical rest when the work has a lull, but under pressure I have a mainline cut-off of everything that represents emotional demands.

It might be selfish and tough for those who live with you but it's very much a case of survival or expiry. If it gets to the point where you must take time off then try to see it as an investment. You *are* your business and you have to take care of yourself.

Personal happiness sometimes has to come before professional ambition until things are on an even keel again. Most people feel acutely guilty about having to do this. But think practically about it. No factory manager would fail to replace a machine with metal fatigue and no company director would fail to replace a person who was no longer effectual. It's you who is struck down with metal fatigue (or, in this case, mental fatigue) or a breakdown in effectiveness, and if you don't ditch your rundown self and replace it with a refreshed one, your business will suffer the consequences.

In this age of enlightenment for emotional and mental stresses, there are dozens of disciplines designed to help you relax, from yoga to keep-fit, from the Alexander Technique to the Japanese tea ceremony. Find one that suits you and make time to do it.

Recognising your limitations

A major aspect in the avoidance of burn-out is recognising your limitations. You can only do so much at any one time. Sometimes you can only do so much regardless of time. Whilst your motto might be *Limits exist only in one's mind*, it is realistic to be aware that there are effectively limits which simply cannot be broadened.

Some people progress faster than others. Those with a sharp money sense, loads of adaptability and gallons of flair might hit the jackpot in a year while you're still plodding along years later. None of us are the same, and having no set parameters for the job none of us know how great their potential for achievement is. There are also many who miss opportunities that would make them surge forward. This is partly due to the fact that many people don't recognise an opportunity when they meet it because it usually goes around in overalls looking like hard work!

Some of us are not destined to go far, staying paddling in the shallows while others swim through the breakers. If we paddle successfully and believe in our paddling, that's fine. It is not essential to take to deeper waters. Accept your achievement and build on it rather than get all bitter and twisted because you're not swimming as fast as somebody else. Competition is a marvellous and healthy thing but no two people have the same make-up or aspirations. Know your capabilities and limitations and plan your forward progress accordingly. That person out there in the waves might just drown. He or she might be having a lousy homelife whereas yours is blissful. He or she might have financial commitments, loans, debts, bills that are sky-high while you have no overdraft or dependents and own everything you possess.

Who knows, that person might have high blood pressure and a peptic ulcer from struggling to over-achieve. Alternatively, of course, he or she might have irresistible charm and be able to sell the proverbial igloos to Eskimoes while you nearly die selling your talented self to already devoted clients.

Achievement is as long as a piece of string. It is wrong to feel cowed when others around you soar upwards. Their needs undoubtably are not the same as yours. If you find their performance impressive, then by all means use them as an example, a sort of mentor to ask advice from or observe. People are usually thrilled to be of assistance, and among the freelance world there is a strong streak of understanding and exchange within the community. But beware of demanding too much of yourself and risking the burnout.

Phil, director of an exhibition construction company, says:

To be on target you need to find the balance between gearing up for greater things before you need to and actually hanging in there never biting off more than you can chew. This is the mid-term phase people don't warn you about, when you don't know how far to go before finding out whether you will sink or swim.

In other cases, to be on target can mean *not* finding the balance at all and risking the lot, biting off far more than you can chew.

Tony Elliott, publisher of *Time Out* magazine, set up in 1970 with £70 borrowed from his mother. This was used to pay half the printer's fee; the profit from selling the magazine on the street was used to pay the other half. At the time Elliott and a staff of three worked on the magazine. For the first three months none of them was paid.

> *None of us could draw a salary. It was only in the fourth month we were each paid the princely sum of £17 a week.*

Elliott and his co-shareholders now own one of the country's most successful publications.

Communication

If the word autonomy ever seemed like an academic abstraction it becomes vivid reality when you're the boss. Autonomy is glorious most of the time, but sometimes it can be ghastly. Either way it puts a totally new complexion on life. Being autonomous is not something we're bred to be despite living in capitalist Britain where, we are told, anyone who tries can make it. Autonomy needs supreme management and communications skills before it can work effectively. Britain is the worst of the industrialised countries as far as effective skilled management training goes. Consequently communication hasn't been focused on and most of us are pretty feeble at getting across what we mean. Far too often in Establishment companies the boss will refer a customer to somebody else 'who will explain it fully', as the boss himself doesn't entirely understand the product/service. He's good on managerial knowledge but poor on technical skills and/or product knowledge (how the lathe works/why a certain approach is favoured, etc.).

If you're the boss, you have to do the communicating. This is closely related to the psychology of self-esteem as you will have to believe not only in yourself but in your product/service. Even if your knees are knocking and nervous sweat is pouring down your back, once you begin selling you are going to have to move into overdrive and do it effectively and efficiently. (See Chapter 5.)

From the very beginning you must think of yourself as a business, which is sometimes hard for artists and artisans to do. Most of us are not very inclined to manage a business. However, we are forced to become our own business managers and success or failure may come to depend on our talents in this area.

For shy people this can be the most unpleasant part of this exciting, inventive and satisfying new lifestyle. Certain fields of operation, like photography, journalism and design, have agents to take the bumps between producer and purchaser, but plenty of spheres don't. The freelancer is forced to become a hustler, a smooth-talking salesperson. This is the time when communication comes to the fore. If it's been difficult before, it is going to be one hell of a problem now.

Communication is all about making yourself clear. It involves clarity, brevity and conviction. It means you have to know your subject, know your opponent and listen (with an intelligent look on your face!) to what he or she has to say. You should never resort to talking down to your client and you should always make them interested enough to want to listen. If you are a bore that person will either switch off or go into selective hearing. Don't insist that you know more than others about the subject under discussion – and let people finish what they are saying.

On the days when you know you've got to go out and communicate try to warm-up in front of a mirror if necesary, so that you appear fluent and to the point. (I always think of an Epicurus quote: 'The greater the difficulty, the more glory in surmounting it. Skilful pilots gain their reputation from storms and tempests.')

Few potential clients have time to sit around and chat pleasantly, so make the message loud and clear: this is my product, it is the best and you need me to make/do it for you. Be as succinct as possible. If you're unsure of how to phrase it in acceptable terms, either borrow one of the many books on communicating from the library (why buy when you can borrow?) or else ask a friend to give you feedback on your proposed presentation.

LEVERAGE

Leverage is the art of moving close to people you rely on and balancing the relationship so that they gain as much benefit from cooperating with you as you do from them. It requires cordiality and communication.

This leverage process turns one-way reliance into a two-way mutual cooperation pact that greatly helps you achieve what you want.

It is a concept which it is essential you understand when you're out there building up your empire. The better the links and leverage points, the better the communication and clear mindedness, the easier it will be to grow.

FEEDBACK

One source of nourishment that helps healthy growth and which is usually sadly missed by the solo worker is feedback. Staffers normally will acquire it, if not directly with words of congratulations or scolding, in a roundabout way in the form of a bonus or rise, or the opposite.

However, when you're outside the circle clients often forget to give you a call to say how nice it was or to drop you a line to confirm their pleasure at the job you did. Malcolm, a journalist, says:

> *You can work on a project for a month, nurture it like your child and deliver it to deadline and the only indication that (a) they saw it and (b) it was good enough was when the cheque comes three months later and you see the job in print.*

You could be very upset by this apparent lack of care, but take a little time off to see how often you give others feedback, even in tiny things like remarking on a new shirt or interesting logo. Most people, especially the self-employed, find lack of feedback demoralising and, at times, rude. Somehow staffers forget that when you're out there on a limb every bit of feedback helps you form an opinion of yourself, an assessment of your work. There's very little chance of being ruined by praise and little chance of being saved by criticism either!

Prepare yourself at this stage to fight through the apparent lack of interest or encouragement. When you are sure of yourself, ignore the advice of others who tell you that your business will not work.

People outside the freelance world do not realise just how unkind they can be with a cursory negative comment or snide remark. While they can work that sort of thing off on a colleague in the office or have a good bitch behind somebody else's back to make themselves feel better, you and your business simply have to stew away in your own juice. Build up rhino-hide now. Thick skin is a marvellous thing as long as there's sensitivity and awareness inside. If it all gets too much, remember that people who suppress tears are more likely to develop ulcers and worse!

Like everything else, in order to grow your own business you need roots. Nothing great is created instantly. Everything has first to blossom, then bear fruit and finally ripen. The root of the self-employed alternative lies in the freelance mentality. It has such a demanding and rewarding set of mental highjinks that it mustn't be overlooked. Once you've got to grips with the mentality the rest should grow naturally. Somewhere, as Norman Tebbitt said as he presented the Industrial Achievement Award a few years ago, a new Rolls is meeting a new Royce, a new Marks is meeting a new Spencer and discussing how their business might grow.

4
PRACTICAL STEPS

For many people the practical side of starting up on your own will be infinitely easier to handle than the mental brainstorming. When you're sure you want to play the freelancing game, your first move should be to find out if anybody will play with you; and if they will, will they pay you to do it?

That doesn't mean finding out at this stage whether you're going to make a million. It means doing market research and feasibility studies and laying the foundations of a self-employed business. It might sound terrifying but one does this normally in life to find out if something is going to work.

James, an insurance broker, says:

> *Market research is the same as buying a pair of shoes. We wouldn't shell out on a pair that didn't fit or were poorly made. In the same way we wouldn't buy a bottle of lousy wine in a restaurant. We'd taste first, pay later. That's what researching the market is about. Elementary testing.*

Market research

Market research is the process of asking potential customers if they would be prepared to buy your product or service and finding out

53

what they would pay for it. Established firms spend vast quantities of time and money doing market research before launching a new line, assessing the scale and durability of the likely demand. You, too, must test your brainchild in the marketplace.

If you have more than one brainchild, test them separately. It only confuses people if you present them with more than one concept at a time. They will tend to think of you as a jack of all trades and may suspect you of being master of none, even if you know you are master of all.

Make sure you have picked an area to work in that you really love. It's tough enough working for somebody else at a job you don't really care for, but to work for yourself at something you don't like is impossible.

You are going to check the market to see if your idea will appeal or not. And if not, why not? It might be so appealing that everybody's doing it already. Your business will only flourish and prosper if there are sufficient customers for the product/service you plan to supply, and you can compete on the same terms as other businesses already in the market.

To sum up, the first step is to find out who will need what you're offering. The prime factors are how many, why, how often, for how long and what will they pay? The next step is to discover how they can be reached. The third step is to see what the competition is.

Theoretically there is always a gap – or a possibility to create a gap – in any market, or a niche to be found for some special approach. In practice this can be a task for an organisation with millions to spend on research and setting up, rather than for a one-man, on-foot, pen-in-hand concern.

Start by scouring through specialist journals, trade sources, newspapers, the *Yellow Pages* and the business directories. Business libraries have market overview reports. Follow up trade associations and attend trade exhibitions in your particular field. Read competitors' published material. Most libraries have access to publications to save you buying them.

Even the notices in corner-shop windows and on community centre noticeboards are important. This way you'll be able to see who is doing what and where.

If you have a product, take samples of it to show potential buyers if possible. If they aren't interested in buying, ask why. It could be the colour, the packaging, the quality or the price. They will tell you.

It can be useful to make up a questionnaire and take it round offices and houses, or stop people on the street. If you are going to visit businesses make sure you find out the name of the person concerned in advance so you can approach tham on a personal basis. A small operator needs the personal contact if he or she is going to impress and succeed. Obviously choose businesses that are relevant and in the area you wish to operate in.

If your product/service already exists but is the only thing you feel you can make a success of doing, start noticing other people's prices. You will later have to work out whether you can improve on the service or undercut them. Do not always try and outprice the existing businesses if you can improve on the idea and give a little 'extra' (like overnight service) and make up the price there.

There are various books on market research available, as well as market research companies (see *Yellow Pages*) who, for a fee, will do your research for you. It is costly, but if you are not sure about your own findings it makes sense to invest money in a professional report rather than risk it in a project nobody wants.

Nothing is lost by asking friends and family for their opinion, but bear in mind that as they like/love you they are probably unlikely to say what they really feel, so their opinion might prove to be not 100 per cent objective. Ask professionals on the patch and cultivate contacts who have nothing to lose by giving you an honest answer. These people might even be potential competitiors. It is not always necessary to admit to your aspirations. As long as you are not deceiving anybody, or brazenly stealing their contacts, there is no reason why you shouldn't study how competitors are operating.

If you intend to run a secretarial service, get all the local price lists, and even use other people's services to see how you could improve on their operations. If you plan to open a shop go to similar shops, especially if they are for sale, as an interested outside party. Ask them about the area, what the good sides are and how they avoided the hazards. Also, find out why they are selling. Location is terribly important. There is little point in opening a bookshop in an area with low literacy. There is plenty of point in opening one next door to a college if you stock the textbooks needed and no other book outlet or supplier is available.

You should find out what plans the local council has for the area.

Perhaps the office you are interested in renting is about to be hidden under a noisy flyover where nobody would ever be able to find you. Or the nice high street you'd like to see your shop on is due to be turned into a four-lane highway with no parking, thus cutting off both your pedestrian and car-borne customers.

Local estate agents will help you find out about the tone and flavour of a place, and the council will be able to provide a community profile of the area. If you have to move away from your own neighbourhood remember the extra cost of travel, postage and non-local rate telephone calls.

If you want to offer a service like an eaterie or keep-fit centre, a school or agency, where people are going to come and spend some time, it would make sense to draw up a checklist.

EXAMPLE: TAKING OVER A WINE BAR

Name:
Address:
Variety of drink/food:
Pricing:

Inside:
Staffing, how many, who?
Shape of rooms:
Number of rooms:
Seating arrangement:
Type of seating:
Entertainment:
Services offered/telephone, toilet, etc.:
Atmosphere:
Lighting:
Access of services:
Heating:
Gimmicks:

Outside:
Any facilities:
Any parking:
What attracts:
What detracts:

Comments:
Type of clientele, etc.:

It is important to start making notes of who your potential clients/ customers are. They are, of course, everybody: specialists, businesses, friends, advertisement readers, word-of-mouth people on recommendation, old clients, passers-by, the pedestrian on the street attracted by your sign, the bored person looking to kill a few minutes.

Observe carefully. Soon you will be able to piece together a possible profile to who would pay money to buy what you are offering. When you come to advertising and marketing yourself remember who it is you're aiming at. Your first impressions may have had a clarity which subsequently got lost within the mass of detail the project involved.

You could easily end up doing market research in perpetuity because it can turn into a fascinating pastime. The value of market research is debated endlessly. Some people reject it, others swear by it. When I went freelance I didn't do any, charging off with no contacts, contracts or commissions. Market research would have prevented me from going freelance at all! Now I recommend it with near fanaticism to others. It is basically designed to minimise the element of risk and, I feel, in most cases, it does.

The next step is feasibility.

Feasibility

While market research was all about seeing if people will pay you for your service/product, feasibility is about whether or not they will pay you enough. Evaluating your idea means finding out if it is going to be worth the effort. The bottom line here is time versus money. Will it be worth your time in terms of financial rewards?

Doing a feasibility study takes in elements such as the size of your cash reserves and your anticipated income (that is the money you think you will earn, and how long it will take to earn it) versus your anticipated outgoings (the costs, overheads and outlay such as investment on equipment, cost of marketing, promotion and advertising, and the interest on any cash you have to borrow).

It is essential that you do this first bit of hard financial planning at the outset.

OVERHEADS

Whether you work from home or at an office you will have overheads. They are probably the most crippling part of running a business. They include rent or mortgage, rates, insurance, extra quotas of gas and/or electricity to heat/light your workplace and run the equipment. There might be regular maintenance, repairs, alterations or decorating to premises to pay for. There are bound to be overheads like telephone, postage, stationery, photocopying, petty cash float, printing, advertising and travel and possibly also employees' (cleaner, secretary, book-keeper, etc.) salaries above your own. Don't forget National Insurance contributions (you pay your own Class 2), private pension payments, bank interest charges and your living costs.

Even if you don't do any business or make any money, overheads will still have to be met.

OUTLAYS

Outlays include capitalisation or investment, which is the amount of money you put into a business with the intention of making an eventual profit. This can include buying premises, acquiring the essential tools of the trade like plant, equipment and stock, and altering premises to suit local (or national) regulations (e.g. installing a fume extractor or fire escape).

Take into account here other essential equipment: buying an answerphone, desk, chair, filing cabinet, typewriter, calculator, kettle, mugs, extra lamps.

You might also need a car or van, a computer or telex. Think carefully before investing precious funds on extravagant image-builders – your cash reserves might not be able to take the strain and could dry up altogether, leaving you beached. If you plan ahead you will be able to pinpoint a time on your Business Plan and Cashflow Projection (pages 62–3) when funds will permit such purchases.

EQUIPMENT

You might have to buy expensive equipment and raw materials. Every business has different requirements. The only advice that applies across the board is always try to get the best value for (available) money to keep the cashflow balance as level as possible.

It might pay you to lease rather than buy outright, and always purchase through HP or on instalments rather than paying the total upfront, otherwise you could find yourself with a serious cashflow problem. Instalments of, for example, £100 a month over ten months are much easier to sustain than £1,000 in one month.

If you're not absolutely convinced that a piece of equipment is necessary, shop around for a second-hand one. The guarantee will be less favourable but it might suit you to go for used plant at this stage. But you could find yourself in a Catch 22 situation where a second-hand model is available at your price, but it doesn't produce fast enough for you to make your full financial potential. It's an old dilemma: whether to get a loan and invest in new equipment, possibly running into the red but being in a position to take on more business, or make a more modest outlay for a reliable but old and rather slow machine which might not be able to cope with demand. You're the boss. I'm afraid the final decision is yours!

If you can provide some references (trade, bank, accountant) you will most likely be able to establish credit-buying facilities with suppliers when purchasing materials. Most suppliers are prepared to offer trade discounts or 'terms', which means terms of payment within 30 days, within three months, etc. once you've established yourself as a regular customer and regular payer.

DISTRIBUTION

Allow extra funds for distribution. If it's local selling there's no problem, but regional, national or international transport costs can be exorbitant.

Mail order is a possible alternative, selling goods direct to the customer from orders made in response to a catalogue or advertisement, or via direct mail which involves mail shots written to specific people. This is usually applicable to highly specialised, high-priced items like motorbike spares or antiques. You pay the postage and include it in the price. Ask the Post Office for details.

The Post Office also has details of the free mail shot available for new businesses and subsidised mail assistance for exporters.

Lists for mail order can be obtained from The British List Brokers Association, Premier House, 150 Southampton Row, London WC1B 5AL, and general information on lists from The British Direct Mail Association, 1 New Oxford Street, Commonwealth House, London WC1A 1MQ.

Home sales can be an easy, inexpensive and sociable means of selling and distribution. Usually the person whose home the 'sale' is held in gets a percentage of the take, and of course introduces many of his or her friends.

PACKAGING

Packaging can be the last straw that breaks the camel's back when you are pricing. A product that costs £1 to produce should not be sold in a gorgeous box costing 50p. Shop around and consult designers that deal in packaging. There are several magazines on packaging available for inspiration.

Costing

Costing is not an exact science about which umpteen books have been written. Different products/skills have different needs. Costing is all about margins, the difference between what your product costs you to supply and the price you can sell it for. It is essential to get it right. Inaccurate costing could put you out of business.

The key words are 'never underprice'.

Price at prices the market will bear and try to push them up by offering something extra. When you cost out a job you have to take into account your labour (per hour), your fixed cost of material, your mark-up, inflation, interest, depreciation and, if applicable, VAT. On top of that there are things like advertising, packaging storage, distribution and selling costs to be taken into consideration. Never underestimate your needs or try to reduce them artificially.

Cost material down to the last pin. Charging for your time should include the time spent getting the order, doing the work, buying the material and delivering the goods. Don't forget that all the while you have been paying your overheads and these will have to be recouped through sales. If your mark-up is too low you might end up making no profit at all.

If you're offering a service like typing, a simple way to arrive at a price is to knock 10 per cent off local prices, but at the same time offer a special additional service. For example, an overnight service or prompt delivery would cost extra.

With some services, such as preparing *curriculum vitae*, or public relations, a high price indicates quality and psychologically reflects your supreme individuality and (they think) superior service. This can be a tough one to cost effectively because you, the price-setter, will have to psyche yourself into thinking big!

Whatever you quote as your rate, it will always act as a base and it will be hard for you to persuade the client to put it up later. Employment and unemployment have always been dominated by the attitude that work is available for those who want it – provided they accept the going price for their labour. Set the going price the way you'd like it to go – up. Trade up; negotiate down.

When asked to give an estimate remember it is only a guide, an approximate price, freely given, which could be totally wrong. Quotes, on the other hand, are legally binding to both parties. A quote is exact, a firm, fixed price. Set out terms of payment, and if you're operating in a field where there are wild price fluctuations you could always add in a clause that this quote is only good for a specified duration.

Shops will most likely charge their customers double the buying-in price. They have to cover their high overheads and risk not selling the item. It is, at the beginning, in your interests to attempt to price realistically to get their custom and then work the price up when they come back for more. This might be quite soon if you prove successful. You will have to explain the rise in terms of increased costs, increased demand or inflation. Whatever you do, do it with conviction.

Expenses can be filed on the invoice or separately. They, and payment thereof, must always be agreed in advance. They are your out-of-pocket expenses so the longer they remain unpaid the more you will drift towards the red. Generally speaking, people are bad at paying expenses promptly. If you are going to run up very high ones try for an advance against expenses.

Expenses include delivery costs and mileage run up doing the job. The AA provides information on mileage from A to B and cost per mile. If you're using public transport think about whether a staffer at the company you are freelancing for would take a taxi or not and charge accordingly. It is foolish to bill 50p for a bus fare when everybody else connected with that particular company would have billed £5 for a taxi as a matter of course. Take the bus, bill the cab fare! Don't overlook telephone calls: charge per unit and cost in something for your rent, the convenience of having a telephone and VAT. For example while a unit might only cost you 5p it is quite acceptable to charge 8p or 10p per unit.

Other expenses can include postage, reciprocals (buying coffee/ drinks, etc. for a supplier/client), damage to clothes (e.g. dry cleaning after doing a messy assignment) and anything that conceivably the client him or herself would expect to be paid back for. I did a story once where the rubber soles of my plimsolls melted. A colleague nagged me into charging for a new pair and the newspaper came up with enough money to buy a pair of handmade mountaineering boots. Another time, covering a fire, about four strands of my hair were singed. I got my first (and, so far, last!) 'designer' cut and set in compensation.

THE CASHFLOW FORECAST

Every new business should do a Cashflow Forecast, which is a chart forecasting anticipated cashflow over two or, if possible, more years. This forecast should tell you about the (anticipated) amount of cash available at the end of each month, when cashflow is at its ebb and when it is at its flow so you can deal with the situation accordingly. It should tell you how long you are likely to be out of funds and at what rate you will recover.

By trying different decisions on paper you can see the financial outcome. Be sure to check the projected figures against the actual figures regularly so you can moniter your progress. If you are trying for a loan from a bank or to attract venture capital, it is understood that a Cashflow Forecast will accompany your Business Plan.

THE BUSINESS PLAN

This is the list of words, as opposed to figures, about your business. It will probably be more accurate than the Cashflow Forecast because many of the facts are known. This is not done just to please the bank manager or potential investor, it is done to clarify on paper your projected idea. Jeanie, a weaver, says:

> Every time I picked up one of those free booklets published by · banks on self-employment they all seemed to say that the Business Plan was the business version of planning your annual holiday. I had to laugh at first but when I went on holiday and saw how I planned things like stopping the milk, holding the mail, getting the cats fed, ordering traveller's cheques, finding tickets, digging out maps, buying a time-switch plug, organising for the plants to be watered and all those endless holiday precautions, I started to think about making my Business Plan.

The Business Plan contains information which is probably already in your head but is much easier to confront square-on when on paper. Consider the following things:

- where you are and where (you hope) you are going;
- whether you have the ability to get there;
- how you plan to do it;
- how much it will cost and take out of you;
- how much you will get out of it;
- why it will be worthwhile.

It will also include details of the nature of your business, your status, plant and equipment, the markets and competitors, premises, feasibility, insurances, objectives for at least for the first year, finance required, and the dreaded Cashflow Forecast.

Voila, un fait accompli! Your business programme and progress are laid out before you.

Having created the enterprise you will have to safeguard it so it can grow (and make you rich, satisfied and/or famous). This will mean monitoring its progress on a monthly basis comparing actual figures with projected ones, and developing your ability to make considered decisions about future moves.

Where will you work?

Whatever you decide to do you'll need space to work in, be it a corner of the kitchen or a 3000 square foot warehouse. Most self-employed people start their businesses at home. The Apple computer people started in their garage in California. Nearly 25 per cent of all British self-employed businesses still operate from home.

The location of your workplace is vital so choose it with care. Location affects cost and image and if you get it wrong you could be wasting your time, energy and money, Kate, a framer, says:

> *I spent three years hidden behind a railway arch where a welding workshop worked night and day. Nobody could find me, and those that did were not that keen to come again. It just wasn't an artistic enough place for a framer.*

WORKING FROM HOME

Anybody can work from home. If you are going to use the premises for a limited company, the law requires you to display a sign to that effect so you will have to get planning permission to do so. You will also need planning permission from the planning department of your local council if you want to do something noisy or smelly, or convert your front-room into a shop or your garage into a factory. Your chances of being granted permission are slim in spite of burgeoning home-based industry. However, there are so many loopholes that even the most monstrous of home-based businesses causing disruptions to neighbours will probably not be given the boot for a year or two. The council is supposed legally to rehouse such outfits elsewhere in the borough which, with those long waiting lists, frequently means that rehousing never takes place. See page 101.

The pros of working from home are minimal overheads, no commuting costs, convenience and possible tax allowances. The cons are possibly needing planning permission, possible rates increase, possible Capital Gains Tax when you come to sell the property you have claimed business allowances on, and inaccessibility to your market.

If you are renting you should inform the landlord. If you are in council premises you should let the housing officer know. If you have a mortgage you should tell your building society; there might be restrictive covenants in the deeds forbidding business, even harmless pursuits such as running a day nursery or guest house.

RENTING AN OFFICE

If you're selling direct to the consumer, be sure to find somewhere people can find you. If your customers are not coming to you then your workplace only has to serve your immediate requirements. It must, however, be suitable, for you, your customers and your business.

In the town centre you will find high rent and rates but an office that will be accessible and have an image. Perhaps you think you can't afford the rent – everyone always tells you not to pay too much rent – but then consider that you might fail because no customer has ever found you. Try to strike a balance. Renting a cheap place is a waste of money if the trade isn't there.

Never overlook the reasons why a place has a low rent. Is there an abbatoir next door or rackety trains all day? Visit the spot at all times of day, even Sundays, and at night, too, to check the desirability.

Check the local tone of people, buildings and social life. As with market research, the council and estate agents will be able to provide you with a profile of the immediate area.

Once you move on to the central office/high street shop circuit, rent, rates and overheads have to increase to incorporate aspects like being central for other services and being easy to find. But if they are just what you need, they will pay for themselves. This kind of property can be found through the commercial sections of estate agents (ask the Royal Institute of Chartered Surveyors who to contact if in doubt), newspapers, the trade press, and word of mouth. Enquire at Enterprise Agencies and Chambers of Commerce.

The implications of taking a lease on a commercial property need to be examined carefully. Many business leases are for 25 years. You might have to pay a premium in order to take over an existing one (plus the rent). The landlord or existing leaseholder will ask for references from you (a couple of trade ones plus your bank and/or accountant). Expect periodic rent reviews. Can you afford to take on such a commitment in the early stages?

It's worth getting a surveyor's report in order to pinpoint future repair costs. If you're buying a lease check the agreement for covenants, for example whether you can sub-let, put up signs, etc. There are a number of different regulations – the Fire, Health and Safety Act, the Factories Acts and the Offices, Shops and Railway Premises Act – which might affect you, and strict regulations cover food preparation, health and hygiene. Your local Environmental Health Department will be pleased to advise you.

General considerations
How much space do you need?
Is location important?
Is image important?
Are there any outlets for lunch/shopping?
Do you need window space?
Do you need a reception area?
Do you need storage, customer parking, kitchen facilities?
Do you need office space as well as retail area?
Is there sufficient light/heating/toilet facilities/water supply?
How much are the rates? What do they include?
How often do you have to pay rent/rates?
Is a premium required?
Check the outgoings – can you afford them?
Does the lease include maintenance?
What state of repair is the place in?
Check legal factors.
Will any government regulations affect your business?

Other considerations
Will your existing furniture, equipment and fittings fit in? If not, have you the money to buy more?
Who will look after the business when you're out?
How far is it from your home? Will there be travelling costs?

INDUSTRIAL AREAS

There is now a good range of acceptable premises available if you look hard enough. After homebase the next cheapest alternative would be space in an industrial zone, particularly one which is part of grant-aided scheme. (Ask your local council for details.) This kind of environment might not suit your business, but a managed warehouse – or workspaces – with a resident manager and communal services like typing, tea facilities and photocopying might.

Workspaces are mainly open-plan and usually located in a converted warehouse or factory. You usually rent, as with industrial space, per square foot all in. To make comparisons between the costs of premises, a relative cost is calculated by dividing the annual rent by usable floor area.

It is doubtful that you'll find exactly what you want so think in terms of compromising and sharing. If you can operate on an upper floor the choice will be bigger. Think in terms of a long stay there because moving is always expensive.

Lists of available space can be found at the local council's development office, Urban and Economic Development (URBED), which specialises in old building renovation, the Council for Small Industries in Rural Areas (CoSIRA) and the London Enterprise Agency. In Government Assisted Zones and Enterprise Zones you might get tax and rates concessions and development grants.

What sort of business are you?

Now that you think you know what it is you're going to embark on, you have to decide what form your burgeoning concern will take. If only for identification purposes for yourself it is important to think this out thoroughly. While the natural choice of most self-employed is to operate as a sole trader, joining up with others in a co-operative, partnership or limited liability company might suit you better.

SOLE TRADER

More than a third of all VAT-registered businesses in the country operate on a sole trader basis. It is the simplest form. You are the sole owner of the business and are liable personally for all the business debts. This is the original one-man band where you take all the profit and get all the loss as well. You run into debt and 'they' can take your house, car, typewriter, the lot.

No legal formalities are needed to start trading as a sole trader. You can set up tomorrow. You just have to tell the DHSS and your local tax office, and you should warn the bank manager because your account is going to have its ups and downs until you find your feet. Your accounts do not have to be audited professionally, which cuts down accountant's and book-keeper's fees. There is attractive tax relief because there are a lot of allowances, so keep good, clear, exact books from Day One. Every work-related receipt is a potential tax write off.

You have to have your name (and trading name if different) and address of business premises on all business correspondence.

The advantage of sole trading is in its straightforwardness in setting up and the full control you have over it. But don't assume that because you've now got a letterhead and a 'business' that it will be any easier borrowing cash. As a sole trader more than anybody else you are going to have to justify your existence.

PARTNERSHIP

Here you own the business jointly with from one to nineteen other people. Each partner is personally liable for *all* the company's business debts, which means that if your partner defaults and swans off to the South of France taking the petty cash float, you have to foot the business's bills, and that includes debts run up by your partner and your partner's share of the tax issued in the name of your company.

A partnership may last a lifetime. It's rather like a marriage, you hope it will work but sometimes it doesn't. It is wonderful to have the emotional support of a partner or partners, but partners can and do fall out. Although a verbal agreement can be sufficient it makes sense to have a Partnership Agreement drawn up through an unbiased solicitor. This covers things like the distribution of profits, what happens in times of loss, objectives and responsibilities, voting rights, capital injection, new partners and getting rid of old ones, what happens if the partnership breaks up. Death or departure of a partner can mean selling off assets to meet taxes, and so on.

Sleeping partners who don't join the day-to-day routine but put in money in return for a share of the profits can also join.

Partnerships, like sole traders, have attractive tax relief.

CO-OPERATIVES

Europe currently has 14,000 worker-owned co-ops. Britain has more than 1,000, a three-fold increase over the past five years. Like partnerships, this is working with others, but in co-ops everybody works for the mutual benefit of the members. The difference between a co-op and a partnership is that partnerships are owned by the partners and can employ others, whereas co-ops have equal partners.

A co-operative is not a suitable business for those with an entre-preneurial or individual spirit. They are not designed for individual profit-making. You have to be clear from the outset why you are choosing a co-op structure as they require full-time dedication from the right people for the right product. A lot of co-ops work success-fully because they are made up of people unable to work on their own who thrive when interacting with others.

Control is democratic, with each member having one vote regardless of investment or labour input. They can either be for-mally registered as a limited liability company or run along the same lines as a partnership. Major political support is now being given to co-ops, so raising cash is arguably easier than it is for the sole trader or partnership. Tax tends to be lower than for conventional com-panies and it is possible to combine the advantages of a partnership with those of a limited company if the mix is right.

The most negative side of co-ops, as I see it, is the inability to make quick decisions as each member has to vote and this inevitably takes time. As Adrian Vinken, director of The Leadmill, a music venue and education centre run along co-op lines in Sheffield, says:

> So many ideological principles can flounder with co-operatives. You don't have time to divert precious energies and intellectual output into sorting out internal squabbles or meet-ings that run for five hours and end up with decisions unre-solved!

LIMITED (LIABILITY) COMPANY

Unlike sole traders and partnerships (and possibly co-ops, depend-ing on structure), limited companies exist independently from their founders. A company needs to be registered by the Registrar of

Companies for England and Wales (or, in Scotland, by the Registrar of Companies for Scotland). It must have at least one director and a company secretary. Papers need to be drawn up (probably) with the advice of an accountant and a solicitor. You can't start trading until the Memorandum and Articles of Association have been lodged with the Registrar and you have received your Certificate of Incorporation which arrives a few weeks later.

If there is a high degree of risk to your business which could involve you in being personally liable for thousands of pounds, being protected by limited liability is an obvious advantage. It becomes a legal entity in its own right and you become the director, not the owner. If your co-director(s), if you have any, want shares and the company is your idea, be sure you keep 51 per cent of shares in the company in order to retain control.

You will receive a salary and probably have share dividends and bonuses, and pay PAYE tax. Accounts must be audited by a qualified accountant and the balance sheet information must be available to the public at the Registrar of Companies. So if you don't want friends, family or competitors to know what you're up to, don't turn yourself into a limited company!

The perks are that you have greater credibility with suppliers, can raise capital by issuing shares and may not be sued personally.

The negatives aspects are that it costs money to set up (£50 registration plus £1 duty per £100 invested in 1987), you need extensive record keeping for audited accounts, you have to have an Annual General Meeting, and the profits are subject to Corporation Tax, which in 1987 was 27 per cent of profits up to £100,000 – larger companies pay more on a sliding scale.

Two other forms of going solo are franchises and buying a business.

FRANCHISES

Franchising is using an established name and paying a royalty percentage turnover to the franchisor. It has become very popular and operates in a wide range of fields. Some well-known franchises are Prontaprint, Body Shop, Laura Ashley, Benetton, McDonalds, Wheelers and Avis.

Franchisors generally recruit through advertisements in the press, at exhibitions or through trade directories. For a fee they grant you a licence entitling the franchisee to sell the product or service in a specified geographic area and provide a package containing all the elements necessary to establish a business. This normally includes their name and supporting advertising, training if necessary, and detailed operating manuals. In return you give the franchisor a percentage royalty on sales.

The risk of failure is less than normal and there is a chance to build your business rapidly as there is less administration and staff teething problems because the system already exists.

BUYING A BUSINESS

One route to quick self-employment is through buying an existing business. The advantage of doing this is that there are known financial facts and figures to go on and you don't have to spend time making preliminary financial projections based on hope and theory.

Businesses for sale are advertised in local, national and trade papers. Sometimes company registration agents have businesses to sell. It is essential to get an accountant to check at least the last three – if possible five – years of accounts for you, and a solicitor to check leases, covenants, etc. The balance sheet will show current assets and debts so you will know the history of the business before you start. Check, too, the council's plans for the area – the business might be up for sale because of some major development which will totally eclipse it.

If it is a limited company the directors' names will have to be changed at the Registrar of Companies. For sole traders and partnerships there are no formalities.

PATENTS AND TRADE MARKS

Get advice on patents and trade marks (from the Patent Office at the Department of Trade and the Trade Marks Registry). These are to protect your product from being stolen or exploited by a rival, even though it can be hard to prove they have used your idea. Both patenting and trade marking cost money to set up.

BUSINESS NAME

Before you start to run your newly-formed company, check that you can actually use the name you want to call it. There are 90 words (like 'royal' and 'international') that can't be used unless cleared by the Companies Registration Office. 'John Smith' doesn't qualify as a business name but 'John Smith Bakery' does. Get the pamphlet 'Business Names – Guidance Notes' from the Department of Trade and Industry. Your name can tell a lot about you. Something like Bricks and Blocks is fabulous for a toy company, but not for a building firm. Remember that names are usually listed alphabetically so A1 Builders will be spotted sooner than Zephyr Renovations.

5
PROJECTING THE RIGHT IMAGE

To make a profit you must sell to customers. The customer is the most important element in your business, for even if your product/service is unique and marvellous, with no customers it will remain worthless. Understanding the needs of customers is the basis of good marketing. Your campaign, therefore, starts with image, the right one and how to project it.

A client learns a lot about the person they are paying by the external image of the business. It makes sense, therefore, to design a letterhead that is attractive, efficient and appropriate. Any leaflets, brochures, advertising copy or packaging can incorporate the same design.

Kevin, an electrician, recalls:

My first letterhead was a disaster. It looked like something from the Inland Revenue! I simply hadn't thought about it. I had printed up purely functional, inexpensive letterheads, on the cheapest paper, in regular, bold, black type. As I developed and became very interested in creative lighting this letterhead was all wrong. I finally paid a designer friend to make me up a subtle one that would engender confidence in the rich home-owners who wanted to pay me lots of money to light their bathrooms so they couldn't see their wrinkles, and kitchens so that they looked like a country cottage – in the middle of Manchester.

It seemed to work: Kevin is now a very successful lighting man. Without wishing to state the obvious, the higher you're going to price yourself, the more taste and 'class' your appearance has to project. Of course, if you are running a used-car business you don't want your letterhead covered with delicate script and dainty roses, as a florist might. Neither do you want a plummy voice on the phone: save that for the beauty salon or directors' lunch business.

Image is that tricky thing that puts the right message across. Sometimes you need to apply a little deception to get it right. The right image should enhance credibility (an essential plus) and inspire confidence in the client – as well as yourself. You have to establish yourself as a person of wit, taste, charm and class. If you have letters after your name or something like a radio programme or book to your credit, get it down there for all to see.

It might help to send a *curriculum vitae* with your approach letter, leaflet or brochure. CVs are a skill in themselves and there are agencies who will, for a fee, write one for you. I genuinely feel, however, that it is only the individual him or herself who can heighten the best points and hide the less favourable aspects of their working lives.

A good CV should start with your name, date of birth, age, address, telephone number, sex, marital status (if you so wish), place of birth and state of your driving licence. The body of the document will comprise your education and qualifications, as succinctly as possible, and your working experience.

I recently read one where the person wrote in after each job what they had accomplished there. For example, 'Working at xyz taught me how to market', 'working at abc taught me about office politics and the sense of humour essential to survive it'. This caught my attention and gave me a much better idea of the writer's personality and talents than a straight list of duties would have done.

Keep your CV up to date and always gear it to the work in hand. If you are trying for import/export trade with China, focus on your trip to the Far East rather than on your experience working as a clerk for a Manchester-based components factory.

It is always useful for the reader if you include your interests and hobbies, whether you're at ease travelling and what foreign languages you speak. Also state your availability and attitude to travelling at short notice, and list references or satisfied clients (if available).

Most of us would never think of going out to sell with greasy hair, sweaty palms and dirty nails. It could be very bad for business. You may assume that people inherently know these things, but I've found, as each new class signs up, that many people have never given it serious thought. Self-esteem is vital for successful projection and the confident image can only come from inside, from you. These are things that have to be worked on, unless you are a super person who doesn't suffer normal human failings like insecurity, shyness or uncertainty. Looking good counts for more than you think.

If you're billing yourself as a super-duper exec./specialist then make sure you look the part. It is commonly known as 'power dressing'. Executive women wear suits, secretaries wear skirts and blouses, media men wear casuals, City gents wear pinstripes. Borrow to look good if you have to, or spend some money on a decent, *suitable* outfit that can be mixed and matched so it will do for several meetings. Don't hesitate to say you bought the shoes on the last trip to Italy or the jacket while in New York. (It really doesn't matter what you say if you do it convincingly!)

If you can only afford to drive a rusty old banger, leave it around the corner out of sight. Glen, a copywriter, says:

> *My car became so terrible it was safer to arrive on time by taking the tube. Sometimes, to create a better image, if the client sees me out I'll flag down a taxi – and take it as far as the tube station! It works wonders for credibility.*

It's not in everybody's nature to mastermind these devious little ploys, but success breeds success and to survive you have to be resourceful.

Never forget basic manners like ringing to thank a client for taking you out for a drink or dropping them a line after the occasion. Never say how frightful the state of business is. The client doesn't want to know. It's a fallacy that people will help those who are down by passing work their way. Why on earth should they risk it? There must be a perfectly good reason why the business is flagging and you can't expect a client to shoulder your problem. If you look and act successful the client will believe you are.

Marian, an accountant, says:

> *I make sure I have a tan in winter so that my clients think I have the funds to go to the Southern Hemisphere for my Christmas holiday. In fact I usually work through Christmas, but those*

who aren't close friends assume I've been sunbathing on some beach somewhere exotic. Instead, I've been on the sunbed.

There is, of course, a risk factor here. You might find that the personal strain caused by all this cheating and conning to make an image is just too much. Wear and tear on the nerves is a well-known occupational hazard of the self-employed. You have to gauge your own strengths and weaknesses. Never be tempted to slit your wrists silently and alone over your cashflow ledger. Trust in fate and have faith in yourself. Something always turns up if you've done the legwork, and when it comes it always seems to come in a rush. Make the most of your success and energy, rather than resting on your laurels when things go well.

Time spent dropping in on your clients when you're looking terrific, or redecorating your office or redesigning your shop window is time well spent. Big companies can contract other people in to work as reps or restyle the office, but if you can't afford to do that just yet, you will simply have to do it yourself.

If you believe you can do it you can. If you have to borrow clothes, read up on buzzwords and tells some white lies to get there, do it. It might be tough but when it works the rewards are enormous.

Marketing

Marketing is the art of promoting yourself. Generally speaking, marketing is anything that helps a company sell its product/service. The essence of marketing is to ensure that you and your advertisements and promotional activities are aiming at the right marketplace and getting your sales message over efficiently and catchily. Lack of knowledge about the marketplace, not getting through to the right customers and incorrect pricing can result in bad marketing.

The first two require straight market research – by now you should be familiar with your target population and the requirements of the market. The same applies to the third point, price. You need to do some careful pricing calculations (see Chapter 4).

It helps if you break down your market considerations into sections. For example, **Product Policy**, which identifies your product and its need; **Promotion**, which is getting its existence across to the customer; **Pricing**, which is telling them how much it will cost; and **Place**, which is telling the customer where they can purchase this product.

Don't forget to allocate enough money to sales promotion when doing your initial costings. Kit and Janet, desk-chair makers, comment:

> *We spent all our cash on making the blasted things and then had nothing over with which to let the world know about it. Consequently we had a 10-week period when our precious product sat in store waiting for us to get a loan, design adverts and market it.*

Don't let it be a haphazard gamble. If you're spending large sums of money producing, allocate a share of your funds for professional selling/marketing. The Department of Trade and Industry have a Support for Marketing scheme which gives firms advice on marketing problems.

Advertising and promotion

There can't be many small businesses in existence that wouldn't benefit from a well-planned creative advertising campaign to help sell their goods or service.

Likewise, if you are out of the Establishment work-force you are unlikely to be headhunted for your freelance services unless the headhunters know of your existence. Nobody will buy your product if you don't tell them it's there.

Advertising is a marketing tool and like any other tool it has to be used in the right way. It deals in the careful creation, production and placing of advertisements. It is essential to get the right ad in the right place for the right customers. James, the director of a customised leatherwear concern, says: 'Half the money we spend on advertising is wasted, but we don't know which half!' If they had asked customers where they had heard of the company they would have known the answer.

AIDA is the currently fashionable yardstick by which to gear ads. This is what it means:

A – attracts ATTENTION
I – arouses INTEREST
D – creates DESIRE
A – stimulates ACTION

Which covers everything a good ad should do.

A good ad should be catchy, memorable and accurate, otherwise you are wasting your time. While newspapers, Teledata, radio and TV are for the bigger budget small business, there are legions of other effective but cheap outlets like local and specialist publications, exhibitions, shop window boards, *Yellow Pages*, signs, mail shots, T-shirts, zippy stationery, business cards, ads on vehicles, and – the least expensive of all – word of mouth.

If you can think up a newsworthy angle or special offer about yourself or your product mention it to the local newspaper or radio. Try to get some editorial features, and write letters to magazines that profile small businesses, telling other readers about some interesting/unusual business discovery or aspect of your work.

It goes without saying that the best advertising and promotion is free. Having a press launch or wine and cheese bash isn't essential. I always cite that splendid woman who was making lunchtime sandwiches and dressed up as a witch and took her Sand-Witches round potential buyers on a promotional run. She triggered a story in her local gazette, was heard on the radio and quickly acquired an enthusiastic clientele.

Doing things like that takes innovation, imagination and guts. You need to tap contacts and watch the changing trends in the market carefully. Strike when the iron is hot.

Contacts

Sometimes you might be selling to someone you know – an old contact on the network – which makes the operation simpler. Remember that your experience is your greatest asset, so make it work for you. Brush up your memories of what happened at the last meeting, who you met there, what the results were, so that when the time comes to communicate you are in full voice, so to speak. Business associates/friends will always be impressed with your up-to-date knowledge of their personal life, like their children (how many have they got?), the progress of their divorce, hobbies, etc. It's easy to get together an index card file and refer to it before phoning or meeting.

It is vital to keep up with old contacts. Nurture them (often very boring), and when you need to don't hesitate to use them. It will probably impress them that you have the nerve to approach them and they will feel flattered that you see them as useful. Everybody likes to feel needed and wanted. Mark, an apprentice cabinet-maker turned antique-restorer, recalls:

> *When I left the man I was training with, I made a point of popping in on him regularly, always telling him how grateful I was for what he had taught me and always asking his advice. He felt quite involved in my little endeavour because I don't think anybody had ever bothered to tell him what a nice guy he was. I didn't feel I was scrounging off him when I asked him to put some customers my way.*

If you have worked for some time with a big company there are bound to be people there who you have helped in the past and who now have positions of power. Don't hesitate to remind them, in the nicest possible way, that they owe you one. If they wanted something from you they would probably ask! The Americans are so much better at this sort of self-projection than the British. They have shelves of books on 'psyching' techniques and skill-sharpeners for the novice. It's the 'getting yours' attitude. If you don't get it somebody else will. In the freelance world there is *always* somebody there waiting to step in if you hesitate. The crunch comes when the person you're trying to sell to turns round and tells you 'no', because one step further down the ladder is somebody as good as you, but younger, cheaper and prettier.

Your contacts will help you to establish a web of relationships with all the people on whom you have to rely. We rely on a network of friends in our private life and it's exactly the same in working life, but as a freelance the results are helping you make money.

Finding work

Many self-employed people do several jobs at a time to begin with – like type or book-keep three days a week for basic income and try their hand at the desired career the rest of the time. It might take some time to discover what you are best at if you're a diversifier.

It suits some people to diversify as it helps them stave off boredom or repetition. While 80 per cent of my income is from journalism, I choose to work half a day a week doing PR for a building company and half a day a week teaching a self-employment course, for variety and to get me out of the house away from the word processor. It doesn't matter much which source the money comes from because at the end of the day it is all lumped together to pay the bills anyway. If somebody would pay me as much to mow their lawn/walk their dogs/clean their house as I can get writing/teaching/promoting, I would happily do it. Ethics have nothing to do with it. Money has the same value wherever it comes from, and when you're in charge of earning it, it doesn't really matter how you do it as long as you do – and as long as you feel good about it and can cope.

Beware, though, of taking on jobs you aren't really qualified to do. If your talents will stretch to produce the goods that's fine, but you can kill off your reputation in an instant if you fail. Freelancers don't get a second chance, if you blow it the client will go elsewhere instead of staying with you and spreading the word.

By this stage you should have done your market research carefully and found out what work is worth doing. You should also have some idea of your advertising and promotion stance. All that remains is for you to go out and find some clients.

If you have been setting up your business while moonlighting as an employee, you should have earmarked contracts or clients who will come with you.

If you are freelancing in the media, you should have come up with some sharp angles and fresh ideas to sell to weary editors and idea-hungry producers and directors.

If you are selling a product you should have assembled your list of buyers and approached them. Other sorts of work might be dependent on finding the right market through the press.

Hustling for work is a personal affair between you and the client. You have to do it in the way that suits you. Power at the negotiating table exists largely in your mind and in the minds of those with whom you are negotiating. Try to gain the upper hand but be ready to compromise. Perfectionists who cannot adapt or lower their standards seldom win, and if they do it's at the cost of their nerves. If you are a compulsive perfectionist you may find it hard to believe that the connection between satisfaction and perfection is illusory.

If you're totally unable to face selling yourself or your product or seek your own assignments, like many writers and artists are, you might have to search (sometimes high and low) for an agent who could do the negotiation (for a percentage) for you.

If you are going to go it alone and do your own selling, expect to spend at least one day a week marketing yourself. That, combined with the time needed for basic administration, may mean that pursuing your chosen career might only happen two or three days a week. All these things have to be borne in mind when pricing out your service or setting a cost on your product.

Selling yourself/your product

You need a passion for excellence to sell truly well. A good product won't necessarily sell itself – it usually takes a good salesperson. Once you've got a good reputation things flow more smoothly in the selling pool, but until then you are going to have to go out and flog. When scouting for new territory, on a clear day you can see forever and on a bad one you can't see further than the end of your nose. Don't sell on those days!

Selling requires the seller to understand human nature in order to get the right relationship with the customer. It's important to develop an instant rapport. You need to present your case persuasively but not overbearingly, know all about the product/service – and those of your competitors – and make the best use of the time allowed. This will probably be about 15 minutes, of which possibly half will be spent in taking off your coat, having tea and talking niceties to set the tone before launching into your selling spiel. This spiel must contain all the information you want to transmit about your product/service, with the most interesting/unique points presented first. Finally come round to terms of payment. Once launched, try to get your point across in 30 seconds. Try to close on a 'Yes'.

Be warned about the 'Yes, well, actually', syndrome. This is when you go in and make, or so you think, a killing. The customer has said: 'Yes, well, actually that's just what we need – ring me in a few days and I'll have my order ready.' And when you ring back it's: 'Yes, well, actually it's a bit difficult at the moment,' and so on! A direct 'No' would really be less of a rejection.

At times you might have to be slightly less than frank, or tell a white lie like 'I have a business making hula hoops', when the truth is you are planning to start a business making hula hoops and are still trying to find interested parties.

Never overlook the importance of timing. Hula hoops sell in summer so start selling them to retailers the winter before. Cardigans sell in winter – get out to sell yours the summer before. Shops start buying for Christmas around August and summer fashions are on sale from January.

A good salesman always sells at the full market price, bearing in mind that everything on the market is negotiable. This might mean starting 'up', asking for more than you want, and trading 'down' (reducing your price) to make the customer feel he's 'beaten you down', or it might be retailing at a set price, as in shops and mail order catalogues.

When selling be sure to set up a meeting with the right person. Try to speak to him/her on the telephone to gauge the tone of the person – formal, relaxed, etc. It will give you an advantage when you meet face to face because you are more prepared for their level of operation. Send your literature in advance so the buyer knows why you're meeting him, and make sure you take a sample, a 'gallant giveaway' (if you can afford to) and an order form with you.

Selling requires charm, assertive body language, common sense, clarity and sheer hardnosed determination. You can also employ quite a lot of positive intimidation of the most subtle kind! Certain products need very specialised, strategic selling techniques (there are numerous books on this massive field). London Enterprise Agency runs Meet The Buyers seminars and certain national newspapers have Buying/Selling sections like *The Mail on Sunday's* 'Signpost' section.

Don't feel despondent if a salesman friend of yours recounts great anecdotes of successful selling while you remain mediocre or unsuccessful in the field. Not everybody is designed to sell. It might be more profitable for you to employ somebody else to do your selling if that is the case. Or take a short course.

You should have researched other similar products on the market. It's a good thing to have competition because it keeps you on your toes and your standards high. Never knock it. It reflects badly on you if you're negative or say nasty things about your opposition. While you might think their product stinks and their salesperson has greasy hair and bad breath, their salesperson might have a nice smile and shut up at the right time while you talk too much and are inflexible. If you're competing for clients, behave like a pro. The sale is usually made *before* you open your mouth.

The potential buyer will probably want to know if you are offering sole agency or will offer a first option to his company.

PACKAGING

You can't force people to buy what they don't like. Find out why they don't like it or why things have gone wrong. It might be the packaging. Always try to design the packaging to suit the market. If your product is something for a functional market, like cling-film for caterers, pack it simply and hygienically. If it's part of the more glamorous end of the industry like, for example, a face cream for a natural product shop, it needs to be packaged in pastel colours using natural, rough weave materials. Try to be different and original. If it catches the eye of the buyer it will catch the eye of their customers.

6

OFFICE ROUTINES AND MANAGEMENT DECISIONS

Admin. – learning to love it

You can't like or lump administration. It's something you are going to have to learn to love. Admin. means sound management and being organised – bad administration is the third main reason, after negative cashflow and under capitalisation, why businesses fail. It's an important and necessary art to try and master.

It includes personnel training and arbitration, office matters like heating and buying teabags, legal matters, safeguarding of assets through charts and surveys, problem solving, decisions, maintaining equipment, project management, negotiation, communication, contracts, employees' NI, employer's commitments, planning ahead and, most importantly, the processing of information, the lifeblood of business.

This lifeblood surrounds your business, serving to give information, receive it, record, summarise and sort it, store and retrieve it, reproduce it and, of course, *use* it by processing it to work for you.

Information is something you should try not to keep exclusively to yourself, in your head. It is something you should write down, collect, amass, nurture, look for, hoard, love, linger over and loathe. Your business structure is the framework within which information flows from the customer through to you and vice versa. It forms the backbone of your working life and has to be handled efficiently to make it effective.

Administration of information and the other essentials that need to be kept under control can take an inordinately long time. Poor admin. means the disorganisation grows, jungle-like. When the time comes to cut it back it is often such a tangled mess that some of it can't be saved. It's like that much-used cartoon of the small-businessman with his head in his hands in an office where filing cabinets burst with documents, the IN tray is awash, the shelves are piled high with files and the phone is off the hook and he is saying: 'The business would fall to pieces if I took the time off to do a course in office management.' Well, my riposte to that is, how can you begin if you don't know where the start is? Do yourself a favour and take time off to draw up a system for your office.

I, as a journalist, spend most of my weekday mornings doing office administration – filing, sending invoices, entering my IN and OUT cashflow book, letters, research, reorganising my elaborate (at times incomprehensible!) labelling and colour coding system, phone calls (local only – long distance are for cheaper rates after 1 p.m.), going to the Post Office for stamps, photocopying, etc. Not one creative word makes paper before lunch. At 1 p.m. I (usually!) hit the word processor when I know the rest of the world is out to lunch and my phone won't ring until they return at about three. It is, after trial and error, my form of the dreaded Office Routine.

Elizabeth, a hatmaker, says:

> *If I didn't start every working day by opening the mail, returning calls logged up overnight, filing and answering letters, before I even think about hustling or making my pro-duct, I'm sure I'd feel adrift half-way between somewhere and nowhere. Everybody needs a routine. After all, we have one in our private life. If I don't have my cup of tea, take a shower, get dressed and eat breakfast, I'd never manage to get myself out of the sleepwalk stage and into the day at all.*

A set work routine helps you get into the right frame of mind, making the day more efficient and giving it shape. It makes you aware of time-keeping so that work does not expand to fit the time available but is done in the time pre-set for it. We are only effectively at peak efficiency for eight hours a day, although most self-employed people subscribe to the Adrenalin Factor, which is about increasing the pace of your life by cramming more into it and taking on more than you should. It might work, but only for a time because usually it will end in burn-out! (See Chapter 3.)

The body and mind need breaks and refreshment to keep going.

Work shouldn't become a drudge of unbroken time so set a few daily rest spots. As you're in charge of your own time, if you elect to take a two-hour lunch-break, consider it a management decision!

There are dozens of management maxims. In my opinion the first and most important is time management, the organising of that scarcest of resources – the hours in the day.

Time management

Start by identifying the major time-wasters. Lack of planning and lack of priorities are up there in the forefront. Haste and over-commitment come close seconds. They all equal management by crisis. The solution comes after you realise that planning might takes time, but it saves time in the long run. Horst, an express-rider, comments:

> *If I didn't plan my day meticulously I would be riding off into the sunset on my rounds every night instead of hanging up my crash-helmet at six and going home. It has taken me a lot of rides into the sunset to realise that.*

Popular time-wasters that have already been highlighted include getting started, procrastination, not following through, and taking too long making decisions (either alone or with others). (See Chapter 3.)

It might help to make a list of known time-wasters and put it up where you can see it clearly – like in front of the telephone so that when you find yourself dribbling on, wasting time by lack of brevity, you will cut your conversation back. (Saves money too!) It will definitely help to make out a list the night before of the *musts*, *shoulds* and *would like tos* that you plan for the next day. It is quite interesting to see how much you fail to do of the essential *musts* and how many *would like tos* are achieved with little trouble!

If you are truly poor about time-keeping, try to keep your own time check for a few days, using a chart to jot down each half-hour what you have done from waking to going to bed. When I set this as homework for my students the majority come back the next week saying they haven't had time to do it. Those that do fill it in inevitably find they have actually worked about five hours out of the eight-hour day. It is a joy to watch them reveal their discovery to the class!

After time management must come people management.

People management

Dealing with people effectively has got an awful lot to do with communication (See Chapter 3.) Whether you're interacting with clients, colleagues, leading co-workers or delegating to employees, being the Big Boss will most likely not appeal to a lot of people. (Remember, you have removed yourself from a system of being bossed.) Whatever the circumstances, you're not going to get very far nowadays if you manage people as though they were your lackeys. A more subtle attempt at leadership goes down far, far better. Leo, an independent publisher says:

> *We used to employ an ex-major, but he treated us like his troops, myself included, so I had to ask him to leave.*

You have to look at your own behaviour in various situations to see why people respond to you the way they do. You might need to be either more assertive or less so. You might be good at giving criticism but appalling at receiving it. If you can develop your own personal awareness, difficult situations and difficult dealings with others might become a lot easier. We can't all expect to have effortless charm or the enviable knack of making a difficult job easy. But we can at least try!

Relationships of any kind run along coordination and group dynamic lines. Handling people effectively means spotting the type the person is. The Boss at the 'think-tank' meeting of employees should be aware of the staff pattern: the shy person, the know-all, the thick-skinned, uninterested type, the highbrow (use the 'yes, but' technique), the chatty, the uncooperative, the positive, the negative and the quarrelsome types. And, of course, the office joker and the persistent questioner who always tries to trap you (pass his questions back).

When dealing with clients, try to put yourself in their shoes. Would you buy this product/service from this person (i.e. you), or would you feel this person (you) was not a particularly cordial, understanding or straightforward person? (See Chapter 5.) Don't be afraid to ask for opinions from your colleagues as to how they think the company – and you – are doing. You might have failings that you cannot see and which could be letting your own company down.

Some people find it hard to delegate; others delegate wrongly. Whether you run a small or large business you must be ready to 'loosen up' on the reins and delegate effectively. It's a combination of sound planning, clear communication and belief in your employees. Try to get the other person to understand the tasks you've chosen and given priority for him or her to do. Brevity, clarity and knowledge have to come into play here.

People love to feel useful and wanted. If your staff do well give them a verbal bunch of flowers or a bonus if you can afford one. Good recognition systems and acknowledgement are worth a lot. If you can evoke a sense of pride in your employees they are definitely going to take a greater interest and do the job better for you. Aside from your own efforts, the success of your business depends almost entirely upon how well you motivate your staff . . . and this does not mean simply paying more money. If you're running a small team with perks like profit-sharing, you're bound to get more heart and soul out of your staff and into your business.

Never ask 'Have you understood?' because most people will say yes whether they have or not. Try to check their understanding by asking *where* they intend to do this job, *how* they are going to do it, *when* they are to begin and so on. People perceive facts differently for various reasons including pre-conditioning. If they haven't gleaned what you're saying the fault may well not be with them but with you and your inability to be unambiguous and logical. Allow time to listen to them. When forming an opinion of them be aware that your assessment may be extremely biased because of your opinion of the other person's job rather than his or her experience or character.

If your employees do something wrong confront them squarely. If they make no effort at all tell them they are slouches and you are not impressed. Never condemn a person on their first mistake. If they make the same mistake a second or third time think about it very seriously before considering dismissal. (See Chapter 7.)

The above advice should help you avoid the situation described in a rather delightful quote by an unknown author on 'The Function of the Executive' (which is you, me or anybody who's employing staff):

> *As nearly everyone knows, an executive has practically nothing to do except to decide what is to be done; to tell somebody to do it; to listen to reasons why it should not be done, why it should be done by someone else, or why it should be done in a different way; to follow up to see if the thing has been done; to discover that it has not; to inquire why; to listen to excuses from the person who should have done it; to follow it up again to see if the thing has been done, only to discover that it has been done incorrectly; to point out how it should have been done; to conclude that as long as it has to be done, it may as well be left where it is; to wonder if it is not time to get rid of a person who cannot do anything right; to reflect that he probably has a wife and a large family, and that certainly any successor would be just as bad, and maybe worse; to consider how much simpler and better the thing would have been done if one had done it oneself in the first place; to reflect sadly that one could have done it right in twenty minutes, and, as things turned out, one has had to spend two days to find out why it has taken three weeks for somebody else to do it wrong.*

General business management

Library shelves groan with books on business management, the hard facts and figures for potential and current managers, and never-ending updates on last year's theories. However, the overwhelming mass of literature in this field is directed essentially towards the larger firm. This is perhaps not surprising since the bulk of managers and employees work for large firms.

Small firms, in my and many others' opinion, warrant more attention than they normally receive. Part of the reason for this neglect stems from the difficulties of access to such firms that both researchers and advisers have come across. This is nicely put in James Curran and John Stanworth's book *The Small Firm – A Neglected Area of Management*, where they point out that:

> . . . because the small businessman often tends to talk a different language than academics and consultant advisers, and sometimes feels that his business methods may attract criticism and even ridicule if exposed to critical examination, he has tended to maintain a distance from them.

In addition, they pinpoint that the pressure of work usually keeps small firm managers from participating in formal management courses, and so, once again, the two worlds remain apart.

Read their book and contact the British Institute of Management, the world's largest management institute, which has much to offer in the form of information, courses and advice. Business management is a vastly specialised topic and what suits one person doesn't necessarily suit another. Devising an inventory control process doesn't apply to somebody working as a freelance consultant employed for their mental knowledge. Product management for that person equals keeping fit as he or she *is* the product. New product planning for that person would be a matter of increasing knowledge, not producing another kind of piston or pivot.

Whatever type of business management you need, if it's applied badly it will hamper success. Management skills necessary for success include marketing (see Chapter 5), operational planning, which involves quality and inventory control, production schedules and flow, cost analysis, purchasing and job evaluation, and financial planning, which is all that stuff that figurephobics hate: figures and money.

Whilst operational planning is extremely individualistic and applies to people in production who will have to design their systems around their specific business (see reference books for more details relevant to your particular business), financial management applies to all of us. The sooner you develop figurefilia (numeracy) the better.

Financial management

Financial management includes raising capital (see Chapter 8), cashflow, book-keeping and accounting. Let's start with cashflow.

Very simply, cashflow is about figures and the ins and outs of your money: where it's come from, when is the best time to spend it and where it's going. Nothing mysterious, just facts about figures.

CASHFLOW AND KEEPING THE BOOKS

Chris, a maker of blinds, comments:

> *Until I became self-employed I thought cashflow was some kind of dreaded disease like AIDS. Every time I met a person who had their own business they'd roll their eyes and sigh 'cashflow problems' as though they were no longer socially acceptable. In reality, it's just keeping a little black book of money that goes in and money that goes out.*

For most freelancers the IN and OUT book is literally all you need. On one page you list the money IN – what you have been paid – and on the other you list the money OUT – money you have spent on expenses like transport, materials, postage, stationery, etc.

For a small business with loads of stock and equipment things will be more complex and double-entry book-keeping, and possibly a book-keeper, will move into your life, but a simple cashbook which shows income on the left-hand page and expenditure on the right will probably do to begin with.

If you list the expenditure in groups, i.e. stationery, transport, postage, reference, motor expenses and so on, it will be easier for you or your accountant to tot up at the financial year end. With the incoming money, make sure the source of funds is clearly written in, plus job number or subject name.

Information and advice on how to control your cashflow is everywhere. Use it.

If you really don't want to spend time doing your own books employ a book-keeper, part-time at first, to keep your accounts in shape. Well-kept accounts will save you money at the end of the year if you're filing tax returns through an accountant. Find the right accountant through either the Institute of Chartered Accountants, who lists members according to region, your bank manager or local Enterprise Agency, if word of mouth doesn't turn up somebody suitable. Never pay in advance for any form of accountancy work.

The person who gives the accountant a shoebox full of receipts will have a hefty bill to pay. The bod with neat books will get away with anything from £150-plus. I was recently told of an accountant who audited the books of a friend of mine's for £80. I personally find it extremely satisfying to pay a reasonable accountant's fee which I know is based on the fairly organised state of my cashbook. An accountant is there to save you money on tax by exploiting all the legal allowances there are before you are taxed on earnings. He is not there to dodge tax for you, and if he does it is likely you will be pulled up later on.

GETTING PAID

Invoicing: If you are running a retail business like a shop you are likely to be paid there and then over the counter, giving the customer a receipt. If you aren't then you will have to send an invoice, listing everything concerned with the project including terms of payment (seven days, one month, on delivery, etc.). If they don't pay on time you have to send a statement, listing all outstanding invoices and the balance owing, repeating terms of payment.

If they still don't pay it is traditional to send a polite but firm note reminding the client of how much it is, when it was first invoiced and payment deadline. If this doesn't work either, write threatening legal action or get a Fixed Fee Letter written by a solicitor (you pay the solicitor a £5 fee) threatening legal action. If the client still doesn't pay up, sue.

Suing: Thousands of ordinary British citizens brought their own cases to court last year and won them – without the help of a lawyer. Suing for small amounts needn't be a major legal action. In County

Courts all round the country the procedure is quick, cheap and simple.

Under the Small Claims Procedure, claims of up to £500 automatically bypass the courtroom and go to the registrar for arbitration. The County Court limit is £5,000. Bigger cases go to the High Court. In most cases the loser has to pay both sets of legal costs. See the County Courts' *DIY Suing Guide* for details. It is as simple as it sounds. I've done it twice and never even left my office, courtesy of bailiffs doing the collecting for me!

Factoring: There is also a new service which has grown up over recent years that helps businesses over short-term cashflow problems caused by non-payers. It is called factoring. This normally happens when you've been so busy you have neglected your book-keeping (why didn't you get a book-keeper in?) and debts have not been chivvied and collected on time. How it works is that the factor pays you (usually) 80 per cent of the value of the outstanding invoice and collects it for himself. Thus you pay 20 per cent for his service and he makes 20 per cent for his trouble (*if* he manages to get the invoice paid).

The advantages are that you don't have to chase the debtor for money and you also save on administration costs. The catch is that the factor will probably wish to investigate the credit-worthiness of your non-paying client, who will resent it. Also you might end up having to pay the factor for his research!

You need to have an annual turnover of £100,000 and an average invoice of £100. Factors can be found in the classified sections of the appropriate press and in the *Yellow Pages*.

7

GETTING IT RIGHT

There is so much information available on the tedious and ever-changing subjects of tax, VAT and National Insurance that I don't want to spend too much time on them but here are some brief comments.

National Insurance

The Small Firms Service has an excellent set of free leaflets on NI Contributions explaining the ins and out of the subject. Partners and sole traders pay Class 2, a weekly rate which you do by direct debit or by purchasing stamps from the Post Office and sticking them on a card. You also pay an earnings related Class 4 sub which is a percentage of annual profits if your profits are over a certain limit. The tax man collects that at the end of the year so you are expected on put it aside.

In return for that you get no unemployment benefit, no compensation for sickness or disaster like loss of arm, etc., only ordinary National Health Services. If you earn very little you can apply for exemption.

A person with a limited company pays Class 1 contributions as an employee, while the company pays a contribution as an employer.

In both cases, it goes without saying, it is your money. *If* you work for an employer *and* are self-employed, if you earn enough you will have to pay Class 1, Class 2 and Class 4! Confused? Find yourself a copy of DHSS leaflet FB2 entitled *Which Benefit?*

VAT

VAT registration is only required after your turnover tops £21,300 (in 1987) in one year or £7,000 in any one quarter. See the Small Firms Service free booklet *Should I Be Registered for VAT?* It is a domain complicated beyond human comprehension and you will need an accountant to make it palatable. While on one hand being VAT-registered suggests to the uninformed that you're a successful going concern (you possibly aren't – turnover is not profit) on the other you can spend a lot of valuable working time collecting VAT for the government.

If you do have occasion for the VAT man to inspect your accounts, never try to bribe or butter him or her up. They are working for the government, not you, and their job is to collect VAT. They can make your life an absolute misery if they take a dislike to you. They are, after all, human like the rest of us!

Income tax

Many of us are confused by tax and tend to shove those buff envelopes from HM out of sight. The booklets on the subject are nowadays better written than they were but are still fairly difficult to grasp. You are, to a certain extent, out there alone with your tax and your accountant (if you have one), for you seldom see the tax inspector unless they want to go through your books, which is bad news. (I hear on the grapevine that only three per cent of tax payers are investigated.) If you keep your accounts up to date and submit regular tax returns, preferably through an accountant, you will probably never meet your tax inspector.

John Bridge, senior lecturer at Southampton Technical College and leader in the small business development movement, comments:

> *It would be tragic for a small business to go under after three or four years because they tried to slip out of efficient tax paying. The system has advantages for self-employed businesses – it's just a matter of finding them.*

You are not taxed on what you draw out of the business for business expenses, but on what your business shows in its accounts as the profits for the period, before deducting the amounts you have withdrawn. The self-employed have various allowances – check thoroughly for your specific ones – which are set against your assessable income. For example your car, office furnishings and fixtures, typewriters and so on are all assets employed in your business. Deductable expenses generally allowed are (in part or full) rent, rates, insurance, electricity used for business purposes, employees' wages, travelling, stationery, postage, telephone, subscriptions and work-related charities, repairs (but not capital improvements), interest payments, professional charges, uniforms, staff welfare, gifts (value not greater than £120) which are advertising the business, bad debts and other delights.

If you are a public relations person you will be expected to keep a plush office, part of which will be set against tax. If you are an actor you might be allowed to put certain things like make-up against tax. You can claim, to a certain set amount, eating out if it was for staff or if you can provide names and positions of (foreign) people you were entertaining who were Buying British. As a primarily showbusiness journalist I file my clothes and beauty expenses, a tiny part of which are set against tax, as my clippings and air tickets to places like the Cannes Film Festival show why I have to compete with Joan Collins!

A good accountant will be aware of these things.

When you set up solo let your local DHSS and tax office know. You have to start the NI subs immediately but you probably won't pay tax for the first 18 months.

Volumes have been written on tax. I swear by the *Which? Tax-*

Saving Guide of March 1986 which is written for idiots and is ultimately a good read, or *The Daily Mail Tax Guide*.

Pensions

For the self-employed there is only the basic State Pension to rely on. If you are self-employed you should have at least one private pension plan. There are good tax concessions in a pension-plan investment and it makes sense to have something to look forward to, although when posed with the question of what happens to entrepreneurs when they get old I feel the answer is that they keep on entrepreneuring to stave off dying of boredom. But having the choice of stopping work to move on to an income from a pension is a better option than working yourself to death.

It is never too early to plan for your retirement. There are dozens of publications on the subject. The DHSS has a couple to start on. (*Retiring?* and *Thinking About Retirement*) and most life assurance companies have pension packages for the self-employed.

Employing other people

When you start out on your own one of the furthest things from your mind is the idea of being an employer, employing staff. As soon as the business starts to spread it can make sense to employ another person, provided you can see a clear way for that person to earn for the business more than you are going to pay him or her.

Apparently almost a third of self-employed people who go solo expect to take on staff within a year of setting up. I find this hard to believe as one in three small businesses folds within the first year. Perhaps that's why.

Even the smallest employer needs to have a passing acquaintance with the current legislation. The problem is understanding just what it is he or she should be doing. Like practically everything designed by the authorities for the members of the public, the rules and regulations on employees are frequently near incomprehensible. Crispin, a printer, complains:

> *By the time you've worked out what it is you're supposed to do you've lost a week's work, the person you wish to employ and your temper. I now avoid taking on people and sub-contract to freelancers who look after themselves, rather than be confronted by the mechanics of employment.*

Employing others is quite a responsibility. It is also quite expensive. Apart from their salary you have to pay an employer's National Insurance contribution. You also have to deduct NI and PAYE tax from the pay of those earning more than a weekly limit. Ask the DHSS and local tax office for pamphlets. You are often better off sub-contracting or wooing a member of the family or a friend into the fold to help out on the details of book-keeping and wages so you can get on with the actual earning activities. If a freelance or outworker can do it, let them. Wherever possible employ a specialist to do a one-off job rather than trying to teach an outsider.

Employees are found through job centres, employment agencies, careers offices and advertisements, or through word of mouth. The Race Relations Act of 1976 forbids discrimination against an employee on grounds of race, colour or nationality, and the much contravened Equal Pay Act of 1970 basically says that you must pay a man and a woman the same rate of pay for doing the same job.

Unless it's very stop-go type of work, you should give a written (or spoken, but this is asking for trouble when problems arise) contract. You are obliged by law to give it after an employee has worked for you for more than 16 hours a week for over 13 weeks. This contract must include:

job title and description;
hours of work;
pay – the Wages Council set minimum wages and the Low Pay Unit will advise, currently, in 1987, the advised per hour rate is £3.00 – all employees must be given an itemised pay packet;

holidays;
grievance procedures;
sickness and illness procedures;
pensions schemes;
trial period/notice required;
disciplinary rules – such as dress and behaviour.

The more you put in a contract the better.

You should be aware of the various laws concerning the employees' right to join a trade union. It might sound anti-self employment to want to join a union, epitome of the corporate society, but many people do or have to. Further, they could counter your grievances against them through their union or through an industrial tribunal.

You are not allowed to sack outright unless the person has worked for you less than a month or is caught in an flagrant act of gross misconduct. Consult a solicitor on firing or the Department of Employment.

The Small Firms Service has a free booklet on *Employing People*.

Licensing

The laws surrounding licensing are a tangled maze which tend to change with the locality. (Check with your local council.) You'll need one to sell food in public and may need one to sell in a street market, door to door, or from the front room. Licences are usually required for caravan sites, ice cream dealing, slaughterhouses, moneylending, cloth dealing and massage parlours (among a colourful diversity of others!). You'll definitely need permission to advertise in the front window.

Trading laws

These laws are aimed to protect both buyer and seller. The law says goods must be of merchantable quality, must be as described, and must be fit for the particular purpose. If shoes are waterproof they must resist puddles. If a jug is unbreakable the customer is entitled to drop it on the floor in front of the seller. If the goods aren't what they claim the buyer has the right to ask for repair or refund. A notice stating that money won't be refunded is invalid in law and disclaimer clauses can sometimes be a criminal offence.

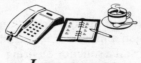

Insurance

If you're in a position where something like the above might happen be sure to have product liability insurance to avoid big damages claims if the kettle you sold should happen to electrocute somebody or if the sandwich they bought from you had salmonella and did them grievous bodily harm.

If customers are coming to your premises take out public liability insurance in case somebody (a third party) is injured as a result of the business's activities or negligence of the staff. This includes slipping on a banana skin and breaking a leg.

There are, however, only two classes of insurance required by law in the UK. They are motor insurance and insurance against employer's liability. The self-employed are known for being under-insured. A recent survey discovered that one in three had no life cover at all and only ten per cent had permanent health insurance. Most also do not insure their businesses, which rather makes the hair stand on end when you consider the consequences of loss or damage to the business premises and contents. Consult an insurance broker or the British Insurance Brokers' Association for details on insurance.

Planning permission

It would be foolish to ignore planning controls and an awareness of what they involve. If your business is going to change the use of your home you will have to obtain planning permission from your council's planning office. There is no hard and fast formula which decides when planning consent for change of use happens. A guideline would be (*a*) if your house is no longer substantially used as a private residence, (*b*) whether your business attracts vehicles/customers to disturb the neighbours and (*c*) whether your business involves any other activity unusual in a residential area. Ask advice from a solicitor if in doubt.

Displaying your name

Whatever type of trader you are, the law requires you to have your name and address visible somewhere at your place of work. You will need permission from the council if you want to display your name outside your premises. Invoices and statements also need these details, plus your VAT number and registered office if different from your place of work.

8

HELP IS AT HAND

There is no excuse for any budding small business not taking advantage of the help available to point the way, either financially or with information. As you expand or become more ambitious make the most of all the help available.

Courses

You don't have to search far to find a course in setting up in business. There are ones you pay through the nose for at private business colleges, ones you pay moderately for at further or adult educaton and extra mural institutes, and totally free government-sponsored schemes which run courses for young entrepreneurs, graduates, the unemployed, people in employment wishing to go self-employed, and others. A little research in libraries will turn up dozens of different opportunities.

It must be remembered that not everybody is designed to be a lone ranger and that many courses are simply a taster to see if the life would suit you. There is absolutely no way a workshop leader or tutor can turn a corporation-minded person into a freelance one. Glynis Young, a small business consultant and lecturer in Small Business Skills for ILEA, reports:

After the first session inevitably a few drop out. It doesn't bother me because I feel I have saved them a lot of time, money and disappointment. If they can't handle the course they would never have made it. But equally this cuts both ways because I can't imagine somebody who is a real live wire entrepreneur getting much out of a course because it would all be too tame in their terms.

In my own teaching, at City University and for the Manpower Services Commission's Enterprise Allowance Scheme, I find that inevitably there are two or three people out of thirty who would be making a fatal error if they pursued a freelance career. Conversely there are also always the ones who tell me I've taught them nothing they didn't know and go out to crash their way into some unplanned business, returning to base to report that they'd been wrongly advised.

Surveys show that in spite of the comprehensive range of courses now available, a remarkable number of self-employed people who have been up and running (i.e. surviving) for a number of years never went near a course and are doing fine.

For example, Richard Branson of Virgin ploughed on regardless.

You simply have to get out there. I can't recall ever seeking advice – I was always too busy surviving!

I remember when I started out in 1978 going with a couple of chums to an expensive one-day course on running a business and coming away feeling terribly confused and rather daunted by terms like profit and loss account, cashflow and overheads, all things that became second nature in due course. In retrospect, I'm inclined to feel that in the early stages the tuition I should have been getting was psychological priming and encouragement plus a factsheet and a reading list to take home rather than being scared off with figures. Generally speaking most people have little knowledge of self-employment before they plunge into the pond. While the Bransons of this world will succeed, course or no course, most of us need a gentle guiding hand to help us along.

James Curran of Kingston Poly, says:

Those who work for themselves need more help. Trainers, for example, must develop suitable packages for this new market of the self-employed. At the moment small business training is going through a honeymoon period but unless trainers can create training relevant to the real needs of the small enterprise owner they are going to miss out on one of the biggest new training markets of the 1990s.

Even a short course must rub something off on the uninitiated, and now that there are so many varied courses it should not be impossible to find one to suit you in some way.

Information

There is no lack of information for those that want it. I would even go as far as to stick my neck out and say there are probably more than enough 'specialists' and 'consultants' on the subject (myself included!) offering help and information. While some are very theoretical bodies staffed by ex-career educationalists and retired big business executives who know the theory but can't be expected to know the realities of life out there alone as a small fish in a giant whirlpool, many information centres now also employ genuine freelancers and small business people who are putting out very sensible, structured messages. Either way they are all supporting the independent spirit that I and many others firmly believe will straighten Britain's bent entrepreneurial spine.

The Small Firms Service is probably the first stop for new students in the self-employed school. A rather cautionary government body which can dampen flair, it has a database, offers local information, advice consultancy on all matters (except legal) and free booklets for new starters as well as existing businessfolk.

Some local authorities have various services for new, small businesses. There are now nearly 250 Enterprise Agencies (Citizens' Advice Bureaux for business) which exist to help people set up and run small businesses and offer free advice and consultancy. Britain has more than 20 Enterprise Zones and eight Industrial Training Boards.

The National Federation of the Self-Employed and Small Businesses has been going since 1974 and is an actively campaigning pressure group for the promotion and protection of the interests of the self-employed nationally. It also gives a 24-hour legal advice service among numerous other advisory sections. Membership is around the 50,000 mark.

The Alliance of Small Firms and Self-Employed People is also a source of enormous support for the freelance business. The main aim of the Council for Small Industries in Rural Areas (CoSIRA) is to help the rural parts of England to support viable and prosperous communities in areas where the population is declining. Further afield the Business Cooperation Network is an EEC body set up to aid small and medium-sized businesses seeking information on an international basis. Wigan New Enterprise Ltd has been set up specifically to promote small business development.

Most banks and even large accounting firms make videos and glossy books on how to do it.

Networks

In the Contacts section (page 157) there is a full list of helpful outfits and organisations for networking and building up contacts, and at government level the Department of Employment is working to build up local networks in a coordinated attempt to make known the diversity of help available through official channels.

Networking has become, like information services, a new-found movement and, for the self-employed individual, a great source of delight. To have open channels of lively communication between like-minded people with that unique freelance mentality is vital. Everybody needs a scratching board to try ideas out on and everybody needs others to exchange news, views, triumphs and traumas. Networks are proving to be clearing houses of ideas, resources and information and they are blossoming like mad. All over the country they are being nurtured from Second-Bedroom Publisher Associations to South Mimms Self-Employed Luncheon Club to City Women's Networks to Ace, the international network for young entrepreneurs.

People are basically gregarious, however independent they choose to be. They need to hear how others have solved a problem or taken a brave step. Jasmin, a PR consultant, comments:

> When I was making decisions about expanding, hearing how others coped with the new status of being an employer really helped me. It also helped enormously when I found the idea of having a massive overdraft more than frightening, but then when I found out dll the others did too I felt one of the gang – a very special gang, too.

By now, many self-employed people are quite a long way down the road. They are not at all sure whether the light at the end of tunnel is an oncoming train or whether it is the big break into expansion.

Expansion

There is now a second generation of solo enterprises, launched on a wave of independent workers about ten years ago, who have not gone under and are quite happily trucking along making a comfortable profit, or at least making ends meet, in the mid-term stage.

But there is a gap in the master-plan that needs to be filled for these people who want help and encouragement to expand and grow. Primary training is fine but it needs the back-up of continued support and solid further training to push the small business person into the big league. Many small firms still don't know where to turn for management and financial guidance, essentials for growth.

At last, a move to achieve a higher profile, in keeping with the Information Age and in keeping with the need for a creative element in business training, is beginning. Most business schools run advanced management courses and several tertiary colleges have part-time evening classes for small businesses who need more information. If you look you will now find quite a few advanced training courses, particularly in marketing and promotion for the established small business person.

The British Steel Corporation, for example, offers a management and advice service, CoSIRA offers technical and business management advice and training. MSC has Training for Success courses. Their Private Enterprise Programme (PEP) is for those up and running and wishing to update their performance. Outfits like accountants and banks are now into much more advanced levels of training as well as their courses for beginners. Many private colleges run excellent courses to push you further.

Networks are proving invaluable here, and so is the increase in sophisticated publications for small businesses which are encouraging many frustrated go-getters who have become bogged down because they haven't planned ahead and expanded. Phillip, a property restorer, says:

> *I desperately need a partner, but I don't seem to be able to make the time to expand and find the right person – or the wrong one either! If I leave the business to the site foreman alone and take time off office work and meetings, then finding other properties falls by the wayside and it's hell catching up.*

In order to expand, to try new ideas and make more money you have to sit back and plan a route which could include employees, partners, more outworkers, larger premises, new skills, products or services.

However, the truth is that two out of three self-employed people do not employ others, preferring to stay a one-person enterprise and handle everything themselves. It is, in fact, virtually impossible in some cases for somebody who is a freelance working alone and living off his or her exclusive skill – for example, photography, copywriting, graphic design or journalism – to employ another. The nature of the operation would have to change and become an agency or a group project. Such people are employed for their individual vision and style. You can hardly be expected to turn out twice as many photos/ads/graphics/articles in order to move into the big league, and clients aren't going to want something done by your sidekick. So your price, as you become more in demand and therefore bankable, has to go up in order for you to make more money.

For manufacturers it is easier, you must produce more goods more efficiently. For businesses like shops and restaurants expanding depends on winning more customers and, if the market can take it, higher prices.

If you can survive the first year, the first five years, the first ten years, you are doing well. By then you should have made a concrete effort to expand unless you are happy with things as they are. Perhaps you are only working six months a year and taking the other six off to do your own thing.

This mid-term period brings with it new appraisals of your business. If you drew up a new Cashflow Forecast it would undoubtedly be very different from the one you started out with. If you made a new Business Plan that, too, would probably be different. Ideas change and energies are re-directed. It might suit you now to tackle just a few well-paid projects a month instead of struggling along working seven days a week getting your name and product/service known. If that early footwork has paid off, you can ease up a bit – but never rest on your laurels. There are always ways to improve your business if you intend to expand or continue to trade with ease.

For me, success has meant having more control of my time. When I have earned what I need to earn each week I take the rest of the week off to do the things I want to. I suppose I could spend that time making more money but I feel richer going out to find stimulation at exhibitions or with friends or away on little trips. It's the touch of the maverick that's appealing!

Raising money

For those who have to raise funds – start-up money – to get going with equipment, premises and stock, it's a matter of going out and finding the money, and currently in Britain there is *no* excuse for anyone to say that they couldn't find funds. Funds are there for the asking for those with a good business plan.

But before we even start discussing how to present a business plan and to whom, I'd like to concentrate for a moment on what it is that is going to sell you – the person – to the bank manager, venture capitalist, investor or any other organisation with the cash readies.

Going on bended knee when looking for finance worked in feudal times when the lord of the manor was the one with the money. Now it is all different. Investors will be on the look out for certain things in you before they'll even glance at your projected idea.

The cleverness of an idea only counts if it can be achieved practically. Which is where You, with a capital Y, come in. Can *you* make *your* idea work? If an investor doesn't have confidence in your human qualities he or she is unlikely to back you, however terrific your idea sounds. Potential investors will only be attracted if you are going into a business venture for positive reasons – to make money by pursuing a market opportunity in a well-managed commercial set-up. It takes courage and determination to create a business that relies solely on brainpower. It takes faith in it and evidence of good management skills to finance it. If you are not up to managing a business you probably won't attract backers, and probably wouldn't survive if you did.

In an excellent ITV programme screened in December 1986, *The Business of Excellence*, the first realistic look at British entrepreneurs, Anita Roddick talked about how you have to be prepared to operate and survive in an alien environment. She warned that you would be carving out your own way through new uncut paths *not* through the traditional channels dictated by your socio-economic environment. To a certain extent people thinking of investing their money in you will want to see some evidence of this pioneer spirit.

They'll also be looking for intuition, that intangible something that frequently goes with people who do it their way. Next they will want to feel certain that you understand what you are doing. After that they will probably seek assurance that you have a good team of affiliates or like-minded people around you for support (moral more than financial). The management team forms the cornerstone of any business. If you are on your own you bear a weighty burden and will need back-up to help you cope in adversity.

Finally they'll get round to the nitty-gritty – cash.

You must know how much you want before you ask for it. The big consideration through the early stages of commercial life will be for working capital, which is money to meet essential outgoings (personal and business) until the cash starts to flow in. This money will cover everything from phone calls to legal fees. It will also foot the bills for tools of the trade, typewriter, telephone, rent, a car or van and office furniture.

Later on you will probably need another injection of funds in order to expand. You might need an expensive piece of equipment or a loan to help you over a cashflow hiccup or funds to buy a lease on bigger premises. Expanding often means more staff, more travel, a better image, and various other money guzzlers. Reinvested profits can help you grow, but they might not stretch far enough to enable you to take a big step forward. However, there is always almost limitless amounts of money hanging around waiting to be invested by people who will put it into something that has the prospect of a profitable return.

PRESENTING YOUR CASE

Presenting your case is all important. Optimism will only go so far in that it shows you have faith in your proposition. But nobody is going to be impressed with anything less than a well-thought case with all the relevant facts and figures to back it up properly and clearly outlined.

It goes without saying you must be able to demonstrate you have a good track record. It is absolutely useless to waste your time and theirs (they most definitely will not have all day) by strolling in to the meeting with no ammunition to fire. This ammunition in the form of a Business Plan, should cover you, your business, your future plans and your financial requirements. As with everything else, this has to be as clear, concise and effective as possible. Expect to be asked searching questions and don't be put off by banker's jargon. If you don't understand their business talk, ask for explanations.

THINGS TO MENTION

You   Your personal commitments, your education, experience, financial connections, reputation and why you chose this type of business.

Your business   The when, where, what and how factors contributing to development and progress, details about assets, possible employees, your market, competition, marketing strategy, cashflow forecast (detailing the first year or two or more, forecasting the incoming and outgoing cash), sales prospects, costings breakdown.

Your future plans   Profits, how they will be made, expansion aspirations.

Financial requirements   How much you would like to borrow, why, for how long, and how you intend to repay it, the security available, valuation of assets and insurances to protect. They will want to know not only where their money is going but when it is going to come back.

When you're drawing this up imagine you're the bank manager or investor. Would you lend money to this person? If not why not?

Approach the investor well in advance of your business's projected start or the time you're going to be strapped for cash. The point where stagnation is beginning to show is too late. Momentum has already dwindled and recouping lost time and reversing negative cashflow is hell. Marshal the financial guns well in advance – it takes ages, sometimes months to organise a loan. Arrange an interview beforehand and send a copy of your details, requirements and/or Business Plan in advance so that the lender is fully conversant with the facts.

RAISING MONEY THROUGH BANKS

With 14,000 different bank managers employed currently in Britain there must be one to suit you. If you can't find understanding from your regular manager, change banks. Like all people in business the manager is only trying to run his bank at a profit. Of course, all but the most unprofessional manager will expect a watertight workability report.

Accountants, solicitors and small business advisory bureaux can help point you in the direction of a bank manager who is sympathetic to small businesses. It's the manager who has to listen, not the bank and if he doesn't fancy being the hand that feeds an erratic small business, he won't lend you money.

Bank managers, it seems, aren't generally top of the pops in the small business community. Borrowing from banks only accounts for 25 per cent of the financing acquired by small businesses. In the manufacturing sector of small businesses less than two-thirds have overdraft facilities and in the non-manufacturing sector (the vast majority) the proportion is less than a half.

Each clearing bank has its own start-up scheme and high street banks usually have packages to help your business get going or expand. Banks usually lend one to one, when the equity capital (your stake in the business, i.e. what you have) is in equal relation-ship to the loan capital (their money, i.e. what you want to borrow). It is called gearing. If they lend you more than you have as equity it is a highly geared loan.

Loans come in various shapes and forms, all of which are detailed in every bank's loan brochures. The most common is an overdraft, which is an agreed limit over a specific period of time with interest (at an agreed amount, usually a few per cent above the bank's advertised base rate) charged on the outstanding balance on a day-to-day basis. Facilities may be withdrawn when external factors precipitate cuts in overdrafts and rates may change.

A bank must have security before it will lend. Security might be a full order book, it might be a house or yacht. It might be good enough to put forward a good Business Plan, or it might take just a good reputation.

If you feel too terrified to approach your bank manager it is possible to do a dry run on a real bank manager via LEntA, The London Enterprise Agency (see page 114).

RAISING MONEY ELSEWHERE

With the social focus more on self-employment there are many, many sources of start-up money other than banks or venture capi-talists. If you find the terms under which your bank is offering finance unacceptable, it's well worth shopping around for a better deal elsewhere.

Start by being referred to an Industrial Development department and/or the Industrial Liaison Office or Economic Development Unit of your council. Ask the chief executive department of your council if they know of any local charities, trusts, grants or loans. Libraries have books listing grants and trusts. Enterprise Agencies (listed in the directory, *Business in the Community*, 227A City Road, London EC1V 1JU) seem to be bursting with taxpayers' money and desperate to help sort out the unemployment problem.

Government aid schemes abound. There are so many of them they justify a service, the first I am sure of many, run by clever accountants, Binder Hamlyn at 8 St Bride Street, London EC4A 4DA. For a small fee they will feed your requirements into their data base and come up with any relevant scheme.

The Department of Employment has a Loan Guarantee Scheme

which provides guarantees for loans that otherwise wouldn't take place and they might pay up to 80 per cent of your loan. The Business Expansion Scheme does a 'wiring job', bringing small businesses together with large companies and is designed to allow up to 60 per cent tax relief for private investors. The Manpower Service Commission gives grants of up to £30,000 to help train you and your staff towards expansion and their Enterprise Allowance Scheme will pay unemployed people £40 a week for up to a year to help their new business. The Youth Enterprises Scheme offers interest free loans for people under 25 and the Youth Business Initiative Scheme will give grants of up to £1000. Shell's Livewire competition has valuable prizes and the Young Entrepreneurs Scheme offers 'soft' (easy repayment) loans. Their Enterprise Loan Scheme offers loans up to £5000 for clients of their participating Enterprise Agency.

The Department of Trade and Industry has Development Areas Cash Grants and loans for industrial enterprises in areas of economic decline and high unemployment.

The Council for Small Industries in Rural Areas (CoSIRA), the main agent of the Development Commission and Regional Development Boards, might help. They also keep information on funds available to small firms setting up in rundown urban areas – apply at the Small Firms Division of the Department of Trade and Industry.

Most life insurance companies will generally be prepared to lend money against 90 per cent of the policy's surrender value and interest rates on this type of loan are usually less than on a bank overdraft.

A little scouting around would turn up a whole lot more subsidised forms of money.

RAISING VENTURE CAPITAL

Venture capital organisations are a growing concern and there are private investors with risk capital (venture – or adventure! – capitalists) falling over themselves to put their cash to the best use. Like the bank they will want to know everything, including what you expect from them and what you are prepared to offer in return (a share, etc.). Take a relatively aggressive stand with potential investors.

You can find venture capitalists through accountants, solicitors and stockbrokers, magazines like *Venture UK* and *Venture Capital*

Report, contacts in the City and Enterprise Agencies like LEntA, which has a 'Marriage Bureau' which links businesses seeking finances with private investors or partners.

Making the most of your profits

Most people find this territory bewildering and if there's any conning to be done, this is where it will happen. How often do you hear somebody bemoan the fact that they made a bad investment and were taken for a fool?

The first consideration is to decide whether you need to invest your profits in the business. It might pay you not to, to keep it offshore (untaxable) or shift it straight into something reasonably long term like a pension fund, stocks, shares or (usually very safe) unit trusts and fixed interest security bonds.

If you think you will need access to your money at short notice stash it away in a short-call deposit account, Post Office account or building society but don't expect to make your fortune on it! Remember, if you are not able to secure an investment which provides you with a real rate of return after tax, your hard-earned profits will actually reduce in value each year. As inflation increases, the more you save, the greater is your loss.

Those who run growing firms sometimes feel reluctant to divert resources to fund a pension scheme, even though they know it is an excellent idea. Stay flexible and adaptable in your attitudes to financial policy. Pension schemes are needed to cater for the future if the present is in good order, and modern executive pension plans do far more than simply supply an income in retirement.

Under the circumstances, however, it might do you better to spend some of your profits on yourself, on a holiday or on something you really want. Here's a chance to boost your exhausted ego by enjoying the efforts of your labours. Things like antiques, paintings and other hard assets like diamonds, stamps, quality jewellery and gold can serve as fine investments to hedge against inflation.

When interest rates on mortgages are low, property investment in most places is generally a satisfactory means to an end. With higher mortgage rates only property in major centres tends to hold its value with high profitability.

The bottom line is making your money work successfully for you . . . and deciding whether you sincerely want to be rich. Like everything else investing involves thought and planning – and luck. Rather than spending a lot of your own time managing your portfolio of investments, consult a specialist in the field of personal financial planning.

Money can't buy you freedom but it can buy you time to do what you want to do. Somebody once said that the happiest time in any person's life is when he/she is in hot pursuit of money, with a reasonable chance of overtaking it. Whatever your reason for desiring to overtake it is, I hope that some of this book will prove an aid to turning your concern into a going one, whatever form success takes for you.

PART TWO

9
FAMILIAR FREELANCE PROPOSITIONS

In the last three chapters of this book I intend to practise what I preach and make you take your first steps along the freelance route, confronting the freelance alternative square-on and encouraging you to do the fact-finding and market research for yourself. Where applicable I give a contact or book reference.

There are dozens of appealing, attractive freelance propositions, and with a few exceptions anything can be trimmed to fit the freelance mould. Whatever way I might outline the job, it will, by definition, be variable. Each potential self-employed person will have their own specific requirements, expectations and abilities, making whatever guideline offered not a hard and fast measure. As individuals you will all make different things of it, as much or as little as suits. Taking a course or reading a book doesn't guarantee results. It is finding out in reality and applying your findings that does.

In this chapter I shall touch on dozens of earners in the crafts, trades and catering, where people like potters, plumbers and candlestick-makers have for many years worked as one-person shows. They are familiar freelance areas which have been described in numerous books (my last one, *Working From Home*, included!) and details are easily accessible on how to get going. If you're interested, go to your nearest library and start reading!

Freelancing in the crafts

The basis of making money in the crafts has been strengthened since (*a*) living 'the craftspun simple life' avoiding 'urban stress' no longer means you have to be vegetarian, pacifist and wear sandals, and (*b*) in the 1980s for the first time craftsmen are being considered as artists.

Dan Klein, the head of 20th Century Decorative Art at Christie's, the first auction house in the world to sell contemporary glass and ceramics, comments:

> *Glassmakers, potters, ceramists and tapestry people, for example, are no longer treated as craftsmen. People now want to buy it and have it in the home or office in the same way they want to invest in paintings and sculpture.*

Not everybody's chosen profession, the crafts can mean plenty to a lot of men and women, whether skilled amateurs or dyed-in-the-wool professionals. I know several people, mainly women who have children and prefer to be home-based, who have picked up a book or gone on a course and now reap fine harvests from one of the dozens of crafts that are feasible. By feasible I mean anything that makes you money, be it the straw dolly contract for Harrods and Bloomingdales or the engraved goblets order for the Rotarians.

Crafts cover an enormous field. Most of the 'softer' ones like needlework, calligraphy, quilting, embroidery, knitting, crochet and macramé require no extra room and no capital investment other than for materials. Batik, candlemaking, glass engraving/etching, caning and basketry, being more bulky, would need a little space of their own.

Others, like bookbinding, enamelling, papermaking, upholstery, jewellery, picture framing, stained glass, leatherwork and weaving will need equipment and perhaps a workshop, although there are no legal restrictions on doing any sort of craftwork at home. However, your domestic insurance policy wouldn't stretch to cover activities linked to earning through craftwork, and if you work from a house that you are renting you should be aware that your landlord has the right to know about it.

If what you're doing creates a domestic hazard like fumes, fire risk, noise or dirt, it make sense to move out to work. You would have to if you wanted to expand your cottage industry into a castle industry. Producing in bulk means extra storage space for materials. For the more technical crafts, the 'heavies' like ornamental metalwork, forgework, furniture making and pottery, the argument is definitely against staying home-based unless you've got a shed or garage at your disposal. The noise, dirt and smell will not endear you to your immediate domestic companions.

With the trend towards inner city regeneration and refurbishment of disused industrial buildings there is an increasing amount of small workshop space on the market, but not necessarily at the sort of rent that a small-time craftsperson starting out would want to pay. For people operating in the country contact CoSIRA or your local enterprise agencies for advice on premises.

Having to find funds for rent will accelerate the process that many crafts people have difficulty with, namely the ability to produce fast. Too often the clash comes between the artistic desire to make a perfect piece which takes for ever to complete and to make a piece that will sell at a price which compensates for the time put into it. It is hopeless to take half a day to make an object which will only sell for a fiver. You have to pay yourself a realistic hourly rate, account for your material costs and cover your overheads in the price.

In craft circles a common cause of frustration can be working alone, cooped up and trying to create in seclusion. There is none of the telephonic or trade interaction that, for example, a chair caner, who collects and delivers the commissioned job, naturally has with clients. If you are making pottery at home five days a week to sell at a Saturday market, the only real contact you will have with your customers is on Saturday. And when Saturday comes and you have to go out and sell your produce after a week 'alone', you can feel very insular and out of the swing of mainstream life. (See Chapter 3 on isolation.)

It's obviously much easier to be a super salesperson when you have a super product. A super product is one for which there is a genuine need – and one for which you have great enthusiasm. It's almost impossible to pitch a product which leaves you cold and not feel like a fraud. Remember, too, that you are entering a field already filled with diligent enthusiasts who do it for love rather than money and have cornered quite a good chunk of your market, eroding away your potential clientele.

You will have to talk to buyers, go to fairs, trade shows and markets and make an attempt to have your stuff included in exhibitions. (The Crafts Council, 8 Waterloo Place, London SW1Y 4AU, publishes a list of shops, galleries, events, fairs and markets.) If you can break into the advertising/editorial world and get your works of art included in the background (or foreground!!) of photographs of house interiors, stage or TV props, advertisements or catalogues you will be moving in the right direction. Imagine everything tagged with an 'As Seen on Television' label.

If you have the ability and facility to teach you gain twofold by having your students talking about you and by possible press coverage because journalists don't feel they are necessarily plugging your product by giving your teaching activities a write-up.

As a craftsperson one seldom finds ads wanting lacemaking skills, whereas the book-keeper and word-processor operator will easily locate a need for their talents in the Services Wanted columns. Use your creative imagination to make your marketing campaign attractive and your product eye-catching. Its desirability might depend on something as basic as its packaging.

It is difficult to advertise your service and the nearest that craftpeople can get to doing that in an effective way is probably by being on the Crafts Council's Register of Craftspeople or their Index of Selected Makers, a prime source of reference for clients wanting craft services.

If you are selling through local markets, flea markets, Women's Institute markets, fairs and fêtes, the location of your stall is vital. The prime location is where you can be seen and got to, close to the passing traffic, maybe near the exit/entrance or the refreshment stand. Make the display neat, colourful and easy to examine, filled with enticing price signs. Don't be shy about asking buyers questions. You can cover a lot of market research this way. Are they buying for themselves? Have they seen similar items elsewhere? How do yours compare? If in doubt of the commercial viability of your proposed business take a trip to London and consult the main centre for crafts, the British Crafts Centre, 43 Earlham Street, London WC2H 9LD, who will tell you honestly if they feel it will be a good little earner or a dead duck that should remain a hobby.

It might also be possible to sell from a home shop or from a craft centre. In America, a successful sales technique has been the equivalent of 'boot sales', where a group of craftspeople create their own 'fair' at one of their homes.

Compile a mailing list of buyers if you can. If a customer has bought from you once and is pleased with the purchase there's a good chance they'll buy again. It makes sense to collect a portfolio of your work, including press clippings and letters from happy customers, and, if you can afford it, print a brochure, preferably in colour, to show to potential buyers and colleagues.

There might also be a more lateral approach to your craft. Elizabeth Bradley found that she had such a good response to her little business of restoring and copying antique needlework that she brought out a range of Victorian animal needlework designs in a kit form which she now sells worldwide.

It had been a mid-nineteenth century craze. Then a few years ago the craze to have Victorian samplers and Berlin woolwork cushions started to grow again and now it usurps all other forms of needlework. Most of the original pieces were in collections or museums but I had a few and managed to borrow a few more to bring out a kit of a dozen different animals.

Her marketing programme included getting special offers in magazines, editorial coverage with excellent pictures of her needlework, and legging it round the buyers at the top end London and New York department stores with samples.

The current nostalgia craze ('Today people are looking at something made in 1981 as if it were archaeology,' says Dan Klein of Christie's) has opened up gaping markets for restored antique clothes – Victorian, Edwardian, Twenties, Thirties, Forties, Fifties and even Sixties – furniture, porcelain, china and pottery, clocks and watches, paintings, cars, juke boxes, everything with an escape-into-nostalgia value.

For all restoration work you need manual skills, good eyes and the tools of the trade. There are many, many courses in restoration (West Dean College in West Dean, Chichester, West Sussex, is probably the largest source of information), but the success or failure of your restoration hangs on experience through trial and error. It isn't essential to take a course if you have a natural flair and are prepared to read up in the how-to books.

Liz Tracy, after she had her second child, borrowed a book from the library on caning and rushing so that she could restore furniture.

I went on until I got it right! Then I tapped into the right market, an emerging yuppy area where they were restoring their houses and wanted furniture to match.

Now she has more work than she can handle.

Peter Pringle bought a book on making silk flowers on a business trip to Japan. He started small, making just for friends. Now he has outworkers and can undercut the imported silk flower market.

Hamish Durran was a salesman for a well-known china firm before he started restoring china.

I knew all the values of the pieces but didn't know the way to mend them invisibly. While still employed I took a course in china and porcelain restoration and repair at an adult education college.

He now advertises in shops that sell china and circulates among the antique dealers to find work. There is plenty about.

Freelancing in the trades

There's money to be made in those services others don't want to get their hands dirty over. Manual work, repairs and activities that are considered to be DIY home pursuits have come into their own. The majority of the working population has never been as well off as it is now. Most own possessions, if not property, and are prepared to pay others to care, protect and repair these assets.

In the past, services like these have been done by either large concerns or the odd-jobbing little men or women round the corner but now, when there seems to be a general shortage of tradespeople, the well-organised freelance contractor is a well-paid welcome addition. Of course a large proportion of the unemployed are redundant tradespeople who can't find jobs and will no doubt be thinking along the same lines as you and starting up on their own.

Work can be found by canvassing your local area, approaching the business there, and advertising in appropriate places like the local paper and in shop windows.

Building, gardening (design, landscaping, clearing), roofing, car/ bike repairs, plumbing, electrics, carpentry, decorating, removals and cleaning services immediately stand out as popular work that can transfer into a one-person show. There are plenty more, like insulation, double glazing, drain clearing, cast-iron work, paving, arboriculture, fencing, carpet cleaning, dry cleaning, laundry, audio-visual repairs, spray painting, glazing and plastering that can easily be adapted to sole trading or the small businesses.

They are all skills than can be acquired, if you aren't already trained. They are also all *needed* skills. There seems to be a perpetual cry for good tradespeople, somebody the customer can trust to do the job while they are away at the office. Somebody who will not rip them off. Expect to be asked to provide references. It helps build client confidence if you show understanding for their anxieties – let's face it, how do they know you're not going to rob them rotten?

Looking in the *Yellow Pages* under Electrical Domestic Appliances – Services and Repair, I found a column of independents who were working almost exclusively from home (I rang up a cross-section to check!) and making a living out of fixing vacuum-cleaners and washing-machines. They told me they had no end of jobs because this sort of work, being considered 'low-grade', meant that it was not popular and therefore not many people went into it. The demand for it, however, is considerable.

Cleaning services, too, are in considerable demand. In fact the whole cleaning industry seems to be taking off as awareness of appearance and cleanliness filters across the Atlantic from the squeaky-clean United States. Businesses are turning to contract cleaners who have the latest techniques rather than using their own staff. On the domestic front the old image of the fag-sucking, tea-swilling Mrs Mop-type char has been replaced by smart cleaning ladies (and men) who arrive looking more chic than their employers and don't want to waste any time on a cup of coffee.

In this category you find empires being built on activities like car cleaning where the state of play has reached the wash, perm, set and blow-dry level. Fidelis Egbudo got a loan from a Youth Enterprise Scheme to buy a steam-cleaning machine for engine-cleaning after his money-making school holiday activities in the carwash field led to him starting up in business. From cars he went to caravans, cleaning them both inside and out.

It seemed obvious to add carpet and upholstery cleaning to the service so I went to Surrey and did a training course to learn all about the chemical side of carpet cleaning.

His jobs range from cars to private homes and offices and he is already on his way, so he hopes, to cleaning up his first million.

Along with carpet cleaning, domestic cleaning and industrial cleaning goes other cleansing work like building site cleaning, window washing, refuse collecting/disposal, house clearances, specialist cleaning like silver, cinema and theatre auditoriums and antique furniture.

My window-washer, Howard, a former employee of a component part factory, quit his job with no qualifications, bought a bucket, ladder and chamois and started looking for windows to clean. He does up to six homes in an area a day, gets paid in cash and spends more time on holiday in Turkey – where he covers his costs by buying carpets for resale in England – than he does up ladders with his chamois.

It made such good sense to me to offer a service that most people can't be bothered to do themselves. I considered gardening but you get really muddy doing that. Anyway I like being inside so I can talk to the people I clean for. Nobody treats me like a navvy and I certainly don't feel that I'm anybody's slave.

With the growing audio-visual market and the drop in the price of commodities like cableless telephones, answerphones, televisions, videos and home computers, specialist engineering services for installing and repairing are increasingly in demand.

With rampant burglary everywhere the market for electric burglar alarm systems, intercoms and security devices is now enormous both within the private sector and the building industry, where homes and flats are more marketable with fitted security. In both cases you will need certain technical knowledge.

In all cases, if you're a good seller and enjoy marketing it might make better use of your time to locate the jobs and put hired workers on the job while you operate as the contractor. Many people are unable to work efficiently for themselves but operate well under a bit of supervision.

Much of the work suggested above is seasonal – roofing is usually summer-work, burst pipes are usually a winter problem, so pro-

vision must be made for the whole year. It might be more conve-
nient to try for a second string in the same field. It would make
promotion and marketing easier if you stayed with the same kind of
work.

It is essential to have an answerphone (or spouse) at home to take
calls made while you're out. Overheads are minimal as most people
work from home but outlays can be high. Many tradespeople need a
van to carry tools and equipment (be sure to insure it sufficiently)
and investing in your own equipment when you go freelance can be
expensive. If you are doing a job that involves expensive materials,
like decorating for example, get half or all of the material's cost
upfront from the client. Cost it out on a job basis not an hourly one
and allow for contingencies. No electrician can foresee a power cut,
no roofer can anticipate torrential rain.

Freelancing in food

Catering, restaurants, wine bars, pubs and cafés are all small businesses that have followed a steep upward trend.

With more affluence in the working population, people are
spending more on their leisure pursuits. Eating out is not a rarity,
cracking a bottle of wine is definitely not grand spending. An
increase in food, wine and leisure magazines has brought out an
awareness of well-cooked food, decent vintage wine and comfortable places to enjoy them in.

Catering has developed into a perfectly acceptable and
potentially profitable thing for a person to do, especially at Cordon
Bleu level where events like banquets, weekend cooking, directors'
lunches, boardroom puffs and dinner parties survive recessions and
depressions willy-nilly. It isn't necessary to be a trained chef, but
unless you are dealing with a specialist service, like wedding cakes,
confectionary, fruit baskets or a deep-freeze cooking service, it
essential to have a good all-round knowledge – as well as love – of
food and cooking.

People are always going to eat wherever they are. While the top end of the market means executive tastes, never overlook the profitability of making sandwiches/snacks for offices, lunch packs for tourists, picnic hampers, simple buffets for conferences or the selling of finished products to food shops, wine bars and pubs, a currently major growth area. While supermarkets stock mass-produced items (like pâté), delicatessens and eateries prefer less easily-obtainable fare and will gladly buy-in new flavours. The same applies to baking. If you come up with a different bread and can produce it at a reasonable price, chefs will be beating a path to your door – provided that they know where to find you!

Food-related activities require specific advertising, like samples and mailshots, to the right people. Because of the nature of the food business the pictures you need to promote your dishes will have to be high quality and in colour in order to make the food look fabulously tasty. The catering business is an upmarket one. It will not pay to have a tatty or cheap image. Reading food magazines will help you find links to the right markets although word of mouth is probably the most effective way of getting known.

For freelance caterers and cooks there are agencies (they charge the client not the cook) to act as go-between. Once established, a popular cook-caterer works on word of mouth recommendation.

Wherever your kitchen, at home or away, it will have to pass a rigid environmental health inspection, meeting the food hygiene regulations on cleanliness, equipment, storage, waste disposal and water supply. You will probably need a large cooker and large deep-freeze. Costs, if you're doing more than a little jam-making, can be high. There is no way the Environmental Health Officer will let you slip through below required standards. If you're cooking at your place and taking it elsewhere the vehicle will have to be fitted to Department of the Environment specifications. And it is absolutely vital to take out a public liability insurance to protect you if one of your tasty morsels were to poison a customer.

It seems to be the dream of many to start a country tearoom or small café. The more ambitious think of opening a restaurant, and in between are the people who want pubs and wine bars.

All those enterprises are going to involve a certain amount of red-tape and official formalities and you should ask your council for details. They also require start-up capital, unless you buy an existing business. Creating a place with facilities like toilets and car park, buying the furniture and equipping it in accordance with Environmental Health regulations is expensive. You will probably have to get planning permission to do the conversion, definitely if you are changing the use of the property. If you're serving alcohol you'll have to apply for a licence, if you're putting up a sign you'll need permission, and planning permission for installing the required loos.

Make sure your market research is watertight and that you've thoroughly thought out your marketing campaign before taking the first step. With a fixed asset like a tearoom or restaurant if nobody uses it or knows about it you are not going to be able to take it to them. Both are notorious for going under within months after the great champagne opening celebration.

Liz Phillip owns two London wine bars, The Archduke and The Footstool. A former librarian hellbent on a career but not knowing what her own thing was, she decided to start a wine bar under the arches near the National Theatre and Queen Elizabeth Hall where, as a regular concert-goer, she could never find a place for a drink at the end of the evening.

I originally thought running a wine bar would be hanging around at the end of the bar having a chat and a drink with friends. But only too soon I discovered it was all about ignoring your friends to unblock loos, see suppliers, stand in for sick staff and wash glasses. It was a rude awakening! With something like a wine bar you can never relax and sit back thinking you're okay. You are part of the service industry and have to be constantly looking for improvements. You can't afford to become complacent. It is, however, a fantastic ego trip to own two wine bars, however hard the work is.

Party organisation fits well into this food and drink section. It is definitely an expanding market, according to those who operate in the field. This is due in part to both halves of a couple working and not having the time (or inclination) to organise their own thrash, and also to the social development of yuppydom and the yuppy's love of parties.

Party planning involves catering and seeing to the drink requirements (hiring in or doing it yourself) as well as finding the entertainer, the disco and video people to film it.

Angie Sharpe, former odd-job worker, formed Jellies, specialising in children's parties, when she was organising a party for her young son.

I started ringing round to locate entertainers and found the choice and price went from nothing to a fortune. Then I began checking on the mobile disco costs and the price of having it caught on camera. Then I checked the availability of caterers and people who do flower arrangements. The range of prices was vast.

At the time I was working as a receptionist in yet another ghastly company so reckoned as I'd never got any job satisfaction from any of the jobs I'd done, I'd put a couple of local ads in the paper and judge the response to a party-planning service.

It cost her nothing to set up as she only needed a telephone and a typewriter. Now she operates from a unit in a workspace in Central London because she needs the space to store the party gear she's accumulated.

Party catering is interesting and rewarding for cooks with imagination. You need a bright selection of divine-looking items which can be eaten neatly with one hand without leaving crumbs all over the place. You might have to go along (or hire a minion to) and serve your edible wares. Unless you have a licence you can't order liquor (get the client to do that) but you will be expected to provide the ice, glasses and possibly somebody to mix cocktails.

Major outlay here is the van to tote all the trestles, platters and provisions to and fro. Potential clients are going to want to see your choice of prices and what they'll get for it. You will have to print a price list of dishes with (possibly) photographs to illustrate. Anything to do with food has to look healthy, fresh and efficiently run.

When setting prices remember that in the end people are happy to pay for quality.

10
THE FREELANCE
SERVICE ECONOMY

The activities in this section are natural hard hitting business ones, the very specialised jobs in what is known as the 'service economy' that have been created by self-employed independents. A growing industry on the business front, they thrive as solo entities. All formerly in-house occupations, they are the services that many firms only need from time to time and now frequently prefer to hire in a flexible freelancer, with fresh new ideas on the subject, to handle the job.

The success of the work depends both on your professional flair for doing it and the stylishness of your service. These are the fashionable 'image' industries and looking good, negotiating with charm, clear objectives and current buzzwords can count for a lot.

Consultancy

Everybody who knows their stuff and has a clear track record can call themselves a consultant. It helps to have been part of a consultancy firm but it's by no means essential. For example, many retired executives set up as management consultants who investigate and identify management problems (and hopefully solve them!). Computer experts who set up as consultants seldom seem to fail in this new, developing industry. Another good, topical area for consulting is the rapidly expanding leisure industry which uses the skills of everyone from sportsmen to social workers.

In consultancy the City image inspires professional confidence. Brochures replace CVs. Smart executive briefcases force out the much-loved but battered leather hold-all. The layout and printing of your letterhead will say more about you than you think. The cut of your suit has to fit the boardroom cloth in this modern branch of industry where face counts and (sometimes) positively silly amounts are paid for services delivered.

It works only if the demand exists. There would be little point being a building consultant in an area where there is restricted constructional development. Most consultants launch themselves with a back-up of contacts acquired while being employed. Often a consultancy proposition is made while you are still employed. Having inside understanding and knowledge, the former staff member will definitely cost the company far less than maintaining a staffer to do it or out-sourcing it to a consultant unfamiliar with the firm.

With consultancy you don't necessarily have to think on your feet. Projects are usually discussed at endless meetings where they are tossed around until thoroughly shaken. Some come clearly defined in report form, others arrive with scarcely a brief. You decide on the time you will need to brainstorm the problem, research solutions, provide recommendations and strategies applicable, and charge accordingly. Fees are per project or per day with expenses charged extra.

The Institute of Management Consultants, 23 Cromwell Place, London SW7, is a good place to start your enquiries on consulting.

COMPUTER CONSULTANT

You have at least to be able to write a program if you are to enter the world of computers, but thereafter it seems that anything goes if you are offering something that is of assistance to the massive pool of people who need help keeping abreast with computer developments. It is possible to work offering a general service or a very specialist service. Most activity is done on the customer's premises although you should have your own computer to put in extra time.

Jobs on consultant level, like all the other forms of consultancy, are through contacts, but if you're approaching the market cold the British Computer Society, 13 Mansfield Street, London W1M 0BP, has information and advice on computer work.

HOSPITALITY CONSULTANT

This much-heralded service is being used by companies who need assistance when welcoming short-stay business associates from abroad. These visitors might need guides, translators, transport, recreation facilities, health provision or possibly escorts. They might have spouses in need of entertainment while the visiting executive is occupied. You will be expected to organise accommodation, meet flights and generally coordinate.

Allied to this is the settling-in type of service which extends beyond helping staff from abroad find their niche, home and hearth. It applies to new businesses moving to an area where they need local publicity, press coverage, advice on local trends and buying habits, help with unpacking stock and setting up offices plus a person to mastermind their opening day.

A carefully worked out mailshot outlining your services should be sent to the personnel manager of appropriate companies and ads placed in upmarket business publications. Fees are negotiable per job.

Information broking

In the early 1970s there surfaced in the world of libraries and information-handling a new service. People who knew their way around the system would, for a fee, provide information and source material from a whole host of outlets. In the old days they would have been called researchers, now they are information brokers or information scientists. Librarians, who understand library and cataloguing systems, obviously make good ones. It helps to have experience in some field of specialist work so that you can bill yourself as something specific, like a nuclear physics information broker.

Clients for information brokers are people who don't have access to information or don't have the time to look it out. They can be businesses, companies abroad, academics, the media, societies and authors. Advertise in business journals and in publications where your line of business is advertised.

Fees are per job and you will be expected to type up in report form your findings. The Institute of Information Scientists is at 44 Museum Street, London WC1, and it would be a good idea if you are a librarian in information broking to belong to the Library Association, 7 Ridgemount Street, London WC1E 7AE.

Marketing

Like consultancy, this is work for somebody who already has experience. Theoretical knowledge is not enough. As already covered earlier in the book, marketing is the strategy a company devises to sell its product or itself. As markets and attitudes change so do approaches to marketing. Consequently you have to stay up to date and be receptive to new trends.

You will be expected to produce a good-looking report, as you would if you were on the company staff. You may also need the services of a market researcher, copywriter and designer, a typist to get the report on paper and possibly a printer to print it.

At the moment, with the increase in small businesses, there is a growing market of clients who are unaware of the importance of marketing and who often come to grief due to lack of it. Advertise in trade journals, sticking to your speciality, and tap old contacts. A chic brochure should show what you're capable of.

The Institute of Marketing, Moor Hall, Cookham, Maidenhead, Berks SL6 9QH, has a directory of members.

Market research

Although virtually everything is now computerised there is still no substitute for clipboard market research talking to all sides of society on all kinds of topics and providing detailed findings on public opinions.

Market research doesn't need any particular qualifications apart from tenacity and stolidness (people can be very offhand at times!) plus an ability mentally to compute the public's attitudes. Even though you might have statistics to prove your point it is expected that you will also submit a full report on your findings. For example, while 76 per cent said they didn't like the product, most of them intimated from their response that they would have liked it better somewhere else, etc.

While you will probably hire in freelancers or students (look for students doing market research as part of their course) at an hourly rate to do the interviewing and standing on street corners for you, you will have to devise appropriate questionnaires, collate results, do research, analyse the findings and prepare the report for the client.

The Market Research Society, 15 Belgrave Square, London SW1X 8PF, has a list of market research companies which you can be listed on, and advertise in appropriate trade journals as well. Look for work by tracking down new businesses or people just starting up in business. Ask the various enterprise organisations for contacts.

Picture research

There are various forms of research needed in business beyond the realms covered by the information broker. Pictures, for one, are often needed to illustrate reports, brochures and exhibitions. Finding them means hours spent scouring collections and photographic libraries and agencies. Or, if necessary, arranging a photographer to shoot what is needed.

Publishing houses, magazines and television have formerly been the main source of employment for picture researchers but businesses with more visual approaches are using them too.

Send your details direct to big budget companies with, if possible, an example of something you have worked on like a brochure. The Society for Picture Researchers and Editors, 32 Bulwer Road, Leytonstone, London E11 1BX, has a freelance register.

Private investigation

Not quite as glamorous as it sounds, this developing service is used by businesses who wish to find out more about potential employees – a kind of industrial espionage, but not so high flying. Investigators are also used to deliver writs, check credit, collect debts and, to a lesser extent, keep an eye on (as in trail) people. Employees who grossly over-use their expense account have been known to end up with a pair of hired eyes observing their champagne lifestyle.

To get work in the upper echelons of top business you need impeccable contacts and a good social profile. Otherwise there is work to be had from solicitors, debt collecting agencies and headhunter agencies. You don't actually need any qualifications but loads of street cred and common sense are essential. Very suitable for ex-detectives!

The Association of British Investigators, 10 Bonner Hill Road, Kingston-on-Thames, Surrey KT1 3EP, publishes a directory of registered members.

Public relations

Lots of old hacks go into PR because it involves writing press releases and it actively requires intimate links with the press and good, obliging contacts who will be amenable to your promotional advances.

The reason one employs a PR or publicist is to get publicity, so if you're operating in the world of promotion you need to look successful and glow with pride for the product you're handling, even if you think it is first rate rubbish.

Most freelance PRs start out by working through an agency as it can be expensive to set up your own PR concern. Like advertising agencies, it usually needs to be a real showcase as it's part of the glossy side of business. PR doesn't stop at press releases: launch parties, press conferences, radio/TV interviews and ingenious or gimmicky promotional blitzes are all part of the job. But the real secret of successful PR is getting your releases published in the right place, your projects featured in the right place, and your customers appearing in the right place.

Most work will be through contacts. With PR in particular you need to be seen in the right places with the right people yourself. The Institute of Public Relations, Gate House, St John's Square, London EC1M 4HD, will advise.

Teaching

Private teaching is something that both the qualified and unqualified do. If you know a subject intimately and can transmit it to a pupil effectively there is no reason why you shouldn't. Much can be learnt by a pupil from somebody who has no O levels but who has a passion for the subject or a lifetime's experience. Many retired teachers turn to tutoring, an activity that requires you to keep up to date with university and school curricula so that you are abreast of current exams. (Working in conjunction with a State school you have to have the qualifications to do private teaching.)

The most regular kinds of private tuition, usually done from home, are music, literacy and numeracy, yoga and allied disciplines, and dance. The demand for English as a second or as a foreign language is still there, particularly the former, and the old perennials, teaching French, Italian, German, etc. are still in demand. The market for teaching unusual things has substantially increased with the public's awareness of enjoying leisure time and realising their full personal potential: private opera singing lessons and fencing have never been so much in demand and the new sports like windsurfing have a market crying out for tuition.

You should, for ethical reasons, get approval to teach your chosen subject from the appropriate governing body. They may want you to do a training course or insist on certain special facilities. They could also advise on where to start advertising your service. If you're working from home advertise locally and in specialist publications as well as at clubs and colleges. There are national education agencies (see *The Times Educational Supplement*) and for something like ESL and literacy your local council should help push you in the right direction.

To teach you have to like people – and people have to like you.

Tourism and leisure

Being a tourist guide has always been a favourite freelance activity. It works for somebody who knows their city, likes people, and takes a pride in sharing the local attractions. You don't need a degree in history or architecture, but merely having enthusiasm for your town is not enough. In London the Tourist Board, 26 Grosvenor Gardens, London SW1, runs courses and you will be expected to do the tour in more than just English. The perks of this sort of work are the tips and meeting a wide cross-section of foreigners. Fine work for genuine patriots!

There are set rates of pay (set by the Guild of Guides and Lecturers) but you could do very well by starting your own specialist tour firm, dealing in specific things like stately homes, Georgian architecture or industrial archaeology. Advertise in tourist agencies, top grade hotels and international magazines.

Leisure skills in Britain are presently in the throes of being developed, not just to help amuse the unemployed but also to keep up with the rest of the world where at the drop of a hat you can find detailed information on anything leisure connected from golf courses to rock groups. Recently universities have started degrees in leisure skills. There are still very few graduates which means that the field is still open for the individual who can pinpoint attractive leisure activities and guide people to them.

Advertise for the foreign market through embassies, tourist agencies and international magazines. For locals try councils and philanthropic organisations that are attempting to improve the quality of life.

Translating

Business and technical translating of the rarer languages is increasingly in demand in Britain, particularly in specialist work such as translating audio-visual parts from Chinese to English or aerodynamic developments from Russian to English, for example. This kind of translation work is better paid than literary work in the commoner European languages, although the EEC has brought more work in the field of commerce and politics. The EEC has also opened up more work in interpreting, a similar, but totally different, skill where you have to translate on the hoof, instantly.

There are no official qualifications other than a perfect written and spoken knowledge of the language concerned and, in Britain, English. The Translators' Association, 84 Drayton Gardens, London SW10 9SD, runs exams and has a register of people interested in literary work and the Translators' Guild, 24a Highbury Grove, London N5 2EA, is concerned with commercial and technical translators.

Mail shots to importers, wholesalers and technical managers of business with multi-national interests, and letters to publishers will probably produce more work than ads in appropriate publications.

Agencies

It's possible to start a viable agency for almost anything: accommodation, cleaning, advertising, babysitting, headhunting, employment, minicabs, travel, information, dating and typing immediately spring to mind. There are always going to be people who haven't the time to find a place to stay or a typist to do their letters and prefer to pay a little more to use the services of an agency.

Julia started a home-finding agency for business people moving to Britain from abroad. Her children had grown up and left home and she had good business contacts.

> *I started by placing ads in the top American magazines that business people read. I also contacted trade delegations, universities with visiting professors and made sure the personnel managers of international companies knew of my service.*

She sent them details of properties with colour photos of the house, inside and out, and grounds if it was in the country. She now has link agencies run by associates in five major centres in Britain.

At the small end of the scale agencies are easy things for people to run from home unless they are dependent, as travel agencies are, on active passing trade and a shopfront to lure them in. If you're thinking in terms of a shop or office overheads will naturally soar. But while the agency can be housed at home it can remain a very low-cost endeavour with high rewards. If, however, there's a constant stream of customers visiting your house in a quiet residential backwater, you might become disliked by the neighbours. Normally the council will only intervene if you are working illegally, i.e. without a licence if you need one.

If the agency involves finding work for people in any way, that is anything from headhunting top executives to hiring cleaners, it will require a licence from the Employment Agency Section of the Department of Employment (2 Church Road, Stanmore, Middlesex).

There is a fairly elaborate web of do's and don'ts surrounding agency-running and as there isn't a publication on agencies, the specifications for each being different, I would recommend visiting a major reference library to look in the Directory of British Associations and the various directories for different trades and businesses.

You will need permission from the Civil Aviation Authority to start a travel agency but nothing is needed to start an import-export one, although export and import licences for certain objects (like antiques or defence equipment to the Eastern Bloc) *might* be required by the British Overseas Trade Board. A marriage bureau can expect to be inspected by the Office of Fair Trading to check it's not a brothel and a building staff agency will be closed down if it doesn't have a DoE licence. These are just a few examples of what the law may demand.

If your agency is going to issue contracts (e.g. for work), acquire legal advice in their drafting, and if it is dealing with people who work for others, take out a professional indemnity insurance against accidents.

It would help if people are coming to you to have a couple of rooms, one for clients to wait in if you're busy, and it is essential to have a telephone and an answering service or answerphone for out of hours enquiries.

Before starting make solid marketing plans as agencies depend hugely on contacts and word of mouth recommendation for custom. Handbills and business cards left in the right places (offices, letter-boxes, clubs, specialist outlets), a press release and catchy, creative ads in guides, handbooks and well-chosen publications will spread the word. If you can find a new angle on your agency, e.g. the world's first agency hiring gold prospecting gear, tap-dancing cockroaches, or skeletons, you will be able to interest the media into giving you free advertising through editorial coverage.

There is no limit to the number of activities that can be turned into an organised agency, or the number of individuals who would like to have an agent acting as the link between the customer and themselves. For many the 'officialness' of the agent who liaises between the two parties is the automatic choice. Agencies are at present one of the fastest growing service industries.

A few other suggestions for agencies include au pair agencies, house-sitting, model, supply teachers, business services, foreign student accommodation, conference planning, publicity, building maintenance, animal-sitting, photographic, news, clippings, speakers, PR, private investigating, nurses, as well as the obvious, agencies for actors, writers, musicians, etc. These last depend very much on knowing the industry in question intimately.

On Valentine's Day in 1979 former actress Beth Owen set up a theatrical agency for artists' voices with a loan of £2000, a trestle table and telephone. Tapping old contacts, she went round recruiting artists in theatrical pubs and clubs to do voice-overs. The agency, Talkies, started with 12 artists. Now with 60 on the books, smart offices in Central London and a full-time staff of three, she owns a thriving limited company.

> *At times it was hard holding it down, but I'd taken a TOPS course in business studies which built up my money know-how and confidence. And once the ball started rolling it didn't take long to clear into profit.*

You hear her voices on a great many of the radio and TV commercials broadcast.

Office work

Moving away from the corporate structure of the agency but staying within business 'service' needs, there are certain freelance activities which keep a low profile but have been part of the scene for a long time. In the past, most large firms have had their own facilities to cope with all of their less specialist, more practical needs, but now, with staff cutbacks, the cross-section of office services like book-keeping, accounting, computer skills, typing and word processing is being out-sourced direct to temporary workers whose fees are still very competitive in relation to charges made by agencies.

As with the Rent-A-Boss scheme, this is proving more economical for all parties and employers are prepared to pay top of the market rates for the particular skill they need. It goes without saying that you have to do the job properly to be asked to do it again. If an employer is pleased with your service – to deadline, to standard and to the latest developments in the field – it is very likely you will be able to negotiate a freelance contract to work on a retainer basis, which places you in the enviable position of having a regular income without a regular boss. Most freelancers in this sort of work start off with their former employer as client and gradually increase their client base by cultivating new outlets through contacts and recommendations. If you have none to start out with then you have to resort to the stone-cold approach with ads in appropriate publications, directories, judicious mail shots or, as a last resort, enlisting with an agency.

Jason Delubi came to London from Newcastle when the company he had been working for as an accountant went under. He had no contacts, nor did he have a full qualification.

As I couldn't audit limited companies' books I set about finding small businesses near to where I lived. I bought a book on small business tax, advertised at the local Enterprise Agency, in shops and the local rags, and scoured the newspapers to keep tabs on small local businesses, particularly new start-ups. I had the help of a contact at the Enterprise Agency. Because I didn't want the expense of an office I would go to my clients, which suited everybody.

Jason has half a dozen regular small businesses as clients and occasionally takes on a new client if times are slack. His earnings are now double what they were when he was on a salary and taxed PAYE.

Like accountancy and book-keeping, secretarial skills such as typing and word processing spill with ease into the freelance world. While typing can be done from home if you have a decent machine, word processing is a pricey business to set up – even the most basic personal computer/word processor clocks in at around £500 – so it's best to work on the client's premises. Advertise locally and watch local developing businesses, although word of mouth is the major source of jobs.

Whilst there isn't much socio-professional back-up for the freelance typist, there is a growing sub-culture of clubs, magazines and associations related to computer users. It's all very much a case of microchips with everything. The grapevine for work seems to be fairly substantial, although computers is one of the areas actually encouraged by management to be done at home. Off-site computer work includes jobs for systems analysts, softwear designers, datapreps, technical authors and programmers and there is a big market for private lessons in word processing and home computing.

One of my students on the City University course, Sue Smee, left her dreary secretarial job to give private lessons in her home on her

Amstrad. After a little market research she discovered that most business courses commercially on offer (as opposed to the higher education or technical college ones) were getting around £100 plus VAT per person. After six classes she was taking on a couple of students a week at £75 for a full day's course with a free phone-in helpline for aftercare service. By the end of the City course, which is ten weeks, she was working a four-day week, surviving better then ever and had her diary full for six weeks.

> *My main source of clients came as a result of going round the places Amstrads were sold, leaving my card and getting to know the salespeople. I also put an advertisement in a small business journal. Salespeople are pretty unversed in these machines and can't demonstrate them properly which means that people buy what is ostensibly just a box of bits with an incomprehensible manual. By the time they've spent a weekend making no progress on their new toy they will pay the earth to crack the system!*

Other business services that can easily be worked independently from home include being a sales rep, telephone message services, address services, duplicating/printing (if you have the machine), messenger service, packaging, indexing and even filing.

I once knew a man who was disabled at 40. Staying at home after a full working life as a salesman was driving him to the brink of suicide. During therapy it emerged that his problem wasn't pain or inability to move but the lack of human contact. He had his telephone connected to the Subscriber's Control Transfer (ask British Telecom) and scoured the local business directory for small business and self-employed people who might want a human answering service while they're unable to answer their phone. His lifeline became playing mother hen to his subscribers, for, of course, a fee.

If you're an office-type at heart and can't bear to quit the humdrum life you could retain a link by setting yourself up as a business providing floral decoration for reception areas/canteens/offices or running the office snack trolley. Wherever groups of people operate there are always numerous human needs and services to be met. Keep your eyes and ears open.

11

CREATIVE WORK

The activities in this chapter have always been a haven for those with creative inclinations. They are the original one-offs, where a person drops out of the oppressive corporate culture to do his or her own speciality occupation in the field loosely defined as arts and letters. This is an area where freelancing is the rule, but life is fairly precarious once you've bitten the bullet. It is impossible to quantify the staying power or business frame of mind of a person involved in the more creative arts as opposed to the person occupied in the more business-oriented areas.

I have tried to group them under related headings.

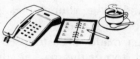

Design

This covers various kinds of design: graphic is the main area, dealing with the design of publications, posters, letterheads, record sleeves, even packaging. Other areas extend to product design, fabric design, industrial design, masterminding a corporate image through a range of designs and book design.

A design training, theoretically, is needed. I know several designers who are making it with their only practical experience gained by working with other designers. They sell themselves very succesfully on impressive portfolios and enthusiastic personalities. This is another work area based very much on contacts, although you can get listed on the registers of the Design Council, 28 Haymarket, London SE1Y 5SU, and the Society of Industrial Artists and Designers, Nash House, 12 Carlton House Terrace, London SW1Y 5AH. Most art schools have design courses and the London College of Printing (Elephant and Castle, London SE1) has a broad curriculum.

Fashion

People are always going to wear clothes and a high percentage of them are prepared to pay over the odds for something different. Britain has more fashion design courses than any other country – there are at least 70 courses currently being run at colleges – which makes for a market pretty well flooded with keen young Emanuel clones. (The London College of Fashion, 20 John Princes Street, London W1M 9HE is tops for advice.)

However, if you have style and flair and a fabulous eye for fashion there is money to be made in the rag trade. If you can design but can't create, farm it out to somebody who can. If you're no good at approaching buyers and selling your clothes, put them in the hands of an agent who will do it for you.

Fortunes have been made in customised clothes, kit clothes, specialist clothes and, top of the market silk and satin fantasies. Accessories like gloves, hats, bags, belts and scarves are good sellers. If you're planning to open a boutique, as about a quarter of my City University students do, consider ploughing in a bit more capital and stocking subsidiary sartorial items like jewellery, handbags, etc. so you can sell 'the whole image', a concept for busy shoppers which has done very well. Also consider the mail order option.

Health and beauty

Health is a highly subscribed freelance area. Apart from the consultants in brain surgery, many doctors and dentists are self-employed. As alternative medicine becomes more accepted, so the opportunities for practitioners to make a good living working at home, at the patient's home or from a small surgery, grow.

To do any health-linked work you have to have trained at an authorised college. Options include chiropody, osteopathy, Alexander Technique, analysis, therapy, nutrition, massage and physiotherapy, keep-fit, yoga, t'ai chi, and numerous allied disciplines with commercial rewards. Check with the association concerned regarding professional guidelines. There are very strong feelings within the clan concerning those not sufficiently trained to be practising and possibly giving a bad name to the others. This is particularly true among the alternative type of healing.

Beauty therapy and hairdressing don't in fact need formal training but most like to see some evidence of training. Easy work for former beauticians and hairdressers, the only snag is buying the start-up equipment like driers, chairs, couches, slimming machines, etc. For those with experience in hair and cosmetics there are well-paid jobs in the performing arts and photographic model styling but they are as rare as hen's teeth. If you can wheedle your way in, hang in there, even doing donkey work to begin with, because it'll be worth the wait.

If you're going to work at home you will need certain essentials like toilet facilities and running water and you should have public liability insurance to cover you if customers are injured during treatment. You might also need a licence. Check with the British Association of Beauty Therapy and Cosmetology, Suite 5, Wolseley House, Oriel Road, Cheltenham, Gloucester GL50 1TH.

The current market is veering towards the therapist going to the customer's house to do treatments. Prices must account for travel as well as skill.

Illustration/painting

Most people in illustrating, painting and technical drawing are trained but if you are truly talented, have contacts, and your style suits, the world is your oyster. It can be a precarious living for the fully-fledged graduate as much as for the talented newcomer. Either way, try to get yourself an agent, a telephone book full of art editors' numbers and an impressive portfolio.

Outlets for people who paint and draw include books, magazine illustration, newspaper reportage, business artwork, animation, advertising, packaging, the crafts such as pottery, greetings cards and wrappings, paintings of people's homes/dogs/children, etc., painting *trompe l'oeil*, furniture, decorating homes with murals, sign painting, frame painting.

Like writing, drawing and painting is a highly competitive profession and an ability to promote yourself, work to deadline and give the client what he wants is almost more important than talent. It will show when you get stale, so take care to keep expanding techniques. The Arts Council of Great Britain, 105 Piccadilly, London W1V 0AM, and the Association of Illustrators, 1 Colville Place, London W1P 1HN, are network points.

Interior design

This is one of the high fashion, posh contact businesses where who you know is vital. If you're in with architects or property developers upmarket enough to use designers for their developments you're part of the way there. If you're in with the rich, better still the *nouveau riches* with doubts about their taste, you're almost the whole way there.

There are training courses, but many successful interior designers are people with an eye for proportion, style and space. You need to know about tones, fabrics, finishes, lighting and texture and also need to be well-briefed on your client's needs. Interior design people usually have a direct line to people who make curtains and loose covers, carpet suppliers and antique dealers.

Very much a word of mouth profession, you can advertise in home and living type magazines. Make sure you have a smart brochure and distribute it round builders and architects.

An *Interior Designers Handbook* is available and the Interior Decorators and Designers Association is to be found at 45 Sheen Lane, London SW14.

Model-making

This is a recently discovered, very specialist field where there's not a lot of room for expansion as young hopefuls continue to pour out of art colleges. There are numerous large model-making companies, and now a sizeable number of one-person bands with an assistant. The range of models required ranges from scale models of buildings for architects to distorted models of miniature/giant oranges and lemons for TV commercials or exact replicas of trees for a fashion ad. Model-makers don't make props and inevitably they are expected to achieve the impossible.

It can be a costly business when your materials are expensive plastics and solutions, and it is essential to work somewhere with good ventilation because of all the glues, varnishes, etc. but then there is a lot of money to be made in model-making.

Adverts in design magazines are the norm but far more success can be had by taking a portfolio around architects, advertising agencies, exhibition organisers and film or television art directors. A Model-Makers Association is currently being formed.

Modelling

There's modelling and modelling: the kind that makes a thousand bucks a day being a cover girl and the kind that is lucky to make that in a year posing in a freezing studio surrounded by art students. The latter, still-life modelling, is soul-destroying work only for those who desperately need the cash. It's not advisable to advertise your service publically as you will automatically be classed in the Young French Model category, so go round the local colleges that run art classes and keep an eye on the columns in art and artists magazines.

The other kind of modelling, either catwalk or photographic is big business for big stakes. I tend to feel that you can't really learn how to have 'it' if you haven't got it – beauty, character, fashion flair and sizzling photogenic style – but training (at private colleges) can bring it out.

For women it's a limited life, until about 25. For men it's longer, possibly into the fifties. Models generally join model agencies who take a percentage of each job they find and will circulate the model's Z Card around photographers, advertising agencies, picture editors and art directors. There are plenty of outlets like catalogue work and exhibitions for good-looking but not exceptional models but the redhot top slots are few and usually fairly brief stints. It's hard work looking ravishing at 6 a.m. and staying that way till the lights die but it's wonderful for the ego when the results are good.

To find work get a portfolio together and start searching for an agent. They will send you round to possible clients where you and your personality will have to clinch the deal. Start by reading *Working As A Model* by N. Household (Batsford).

Photography

Photography, like writing, is one of those pastimes everybody dreams of doing well. Like any other form of work it requires more than just an artistic eye and romantic soul, particularly as there are lots of very good amateurs who will gladly have their pictures used for no payment.

Start-up costs are high as you need a good camera, lenses, flash and lights. On top of that there is processing, which you don't have to do in your own studio but will have to have done to the highest standards at a processing laboratory.

Most photographers start work as an assistant to an established photographer. The fees are low but the experience is invaluable – as are the contacts. Once you've done your footwork and feel you can come up with the goods, try not to bill yourself as a generalist as people can't pigeonhole you as right for a certain job. If you enjoy news that's one thing. If you like advertising imagery that's another. If you prefer the more tranquil lensing in, for example, botany, try to make your mark there. Stick to the area you're best at. If you can get your pictures in an exhibition pull out all the stops to do so.

Before you'll be able to sell yourself you will have to have a portfolio of exceptional pictures – the world is packed with talented enthusiasts – to tote round the picture editors and art directors in your vicinity. *The Writers' and Artists' Yearbook* (A. & C. Black) and *Creative Handbook* (Creative Handbook) list them and the Bureau of Freelance Photographers, Focus House, 497 Green Lanes, London N13 4BP, can also advise.

Fees are usually per job although selling a one-off will be paid as per the rates of the publication for one usage of that picture. Many clients try for full syndication rights on your photographs, which means you sell them the picture outright for all territories. Always insist on a by-line on a published photograph.

Publishing

This is one of the leading professions where freelancing is acceptable, even encouraged. Publishing doesn't only involve producing books like novels, or this sort of book. It also includes the production of manuals, textbooks, company tomes, guides, and private individuals' dreams, as in vanity publishing, among others.

There are various branches of work in publishing: reading manuscripts, copy editing, designing, typesetting, proof-reading, picture research, indexing and paste-up. Publishers will tend towards staff they know can handle a specific subject. There is little point in giving a cookery book to a motorbike specialist for copy editing.

People with degrees in literature are not necessarily more desirable in this field than people without. There are various courses on aspects of publishing. Previous experience obviously helps but if you can set yourself up as a reliable, punctual worker that produces the goods there is no secret code that can't be cracked. Publishing is picking up again after the recent depression and around 50,000 books a year are being published in Britain. The Mark Longman Library at the Book House Training Centre, 45 East Hill, London SW18, specialises in books on publishing and *The Bookseller* is the publishing bible. The Publishers Association, 19 Bedford Square, London WC1B 3HJ, can advise.

Restoring antiques

The market for antiques has never been so big and people are inclined more and more to invest their money in these status valuables. Consequently there are less and less floating around waiting to be claimed and the price of antiques holds up well.

For restoration you need knowledge, manual skills and an ability to do perfect repairs that don't show. If you're restoring a customer's priceless heirloom it's important to write a brief report of what was verbally agreed. He will want an estimate and try to get him to sign a form exonerating you from liability if his Louis XV chair falls to pieces in your hands instead of his. You should, ideally, have your own insurance against liability.

Much antique restoration work comes via dealers, which involves a different approach to the one taken for the personal clients who brings in a much-loved part of the family history. Dealers will want as good a job as possible done in the least possible time for the most moderate fee. The week-long job done lovingly and meticulously will not be appreciated if what they wanted was a quick patch-up job.

This is very specialist work for an enthusiast and a person who knows about wood, finishes, paints, styles and fabrics. Most dealers have runners who pick up antiques from shops, auctions, fairs and backwoods farms around the country. It makes sense for the free-lance restorer to start buying up their own antiques to market themselves through antiques fairs and markets. There are dozens of books on furniture restoration and various courses available through adult education classes.

Go round dealers to promote your service and advertise in homes and antiques magazines.

Writing and journalism

The desire to write, more specifically the desire to write a best-seller, must be one of the world's most popular sentiments. But never confuse the inclination with the actuality. Writing and free-lance journalism are solitary pastimes done by a vast number of people who feel compelled to see their name in print. It is not something that comes to you, muselike. It's work that has to be done to deadline, regularly and to certain standards. If you're doing a piece for a women's page you are hardly going to pen it in the same style as you would a feature on microchips for a computer digest or a poem for a literary journal.

Writing books is one thing, journalism another. In Britain there are 8,000 professional authors of which probably no more than 50 of them will make a 'best-selling' living Catherine Cookson or Jeffrey Archer-style. A large proportion of these authors write non-fiction.

To get a book published it is easier if you do it through an agent who will present your manuscript to publishers. They will take a percentage of the royalties. Finding an agent (see *Writers and Artists Yearbook*) means having an idea and either writing a manuscript on spec or doing a watertight synopsis and sample chapter or two.

There are various outlets for freelance journalism: newspapers, magazines, radio and TV work. It helps enormously to have worked within the fold to create contacts and be able to say that you have worked with such-and-such an editor, because however good your writing is many features editors simply don't have the time to read everything that reaches their desk.

A quick way to get into the circle is to write about something unique, like riding across Paraguay on a camel or about interesting and illuminating developments in nuclear waste disposal, a subject you have been researching for your own interest for months. Being on the spot for a news item is sheer luck and should be exploited. Start by tackling the local newspapers or the specialist magazines where your knowledge on the subject is greater than the average journalist. Send round your clippings and a list of ideas for possible features to features editors (*Writers and Artists Yearbook* again). With so many newspapers cutting back on staff it is currently a freelancers' market. It will probably, however, be tough breaking into it if you are an unknown, so perseverance is the keyword here.

The National Union of Journalists sets rates that no publications seem to keep to. Usually it is per 1,000 words and getting a 'kill fee' for something they asked for and rejected can mean you put yourself in a bad light. At the start you are lucky to get into print at all!

If you get known for delivering acceptable goods on time you are half-way there. Often keeping to deadline can be as vital as brilliant writing.

The NUJ Freelance Branch (314 Gray's Inn Road, London WC1X 8DP) has a *Who's Who in Freelance Journalism*. I've been on it for ages and never received one enquiry. Read also *The Freelance Writers' Handbook* by Paul Kerton (Hamlyn) and *An Authors' Handbook* by David Bolt (Piatkus Books).

Last word – the performing arts

I have specifically avoided mentioning the performing arts because I feel these are such magic circle forms of work that if you aren't already in there you are going to have to have an exceptional talent to make it.

Most actors, singers, musicians, jugglers, dancers, stunt people, magicians and so on are self-employed people. Many spend much of their lives 'resting' between jobs. About five per cent make it big and reap the rewards of the entertainment industry. The lifestyle is probably the most precarious of all the freelance alternatives and very specialist training and advice should be sought if you intend to make your solo way in the performing arts.

CONTACTS

For advice and counselling

Alliance of Small Firms and Self-Employed People,
  279 Church Road, London SE19 2QQ

Association of British Chambers of Commerce,
  212A Shaftesbury Avenue, London WC2H 8EW

Association of Certified Accountants.
  29 Lincoln's Inn Fields, London WC2

Association of Independent Businesses,
  Trowbray House, 108 Weston Street, London SW1 3QB

British Franchise Association,
  75A Bell Street, Henley on Thames, Oxon RG9 2BD

Companies House (Registrar of Companies – England and Wales),
  Crown Way, Maindy, Cardiff CF4 3UZ

Companies Registration Office (Register of Companies –
    Scotland),
  102 George Street, Edinburgh EH2 3DJ

Cooperative Development Agency,
  Broadmead House, 21 Panton Street, London SW1

Council for Small Industries in Rural Areas (CoSIRA),
  11 Cowley Street, London SW1P 3NA

Department of Trade and Industry,
  telephone Freephone 2444

Enterprise Agencies, Development Boards and Small Firms
    Service,
  telephone Freephone Enterprise and ask for local office

Forum of Private Business,
  Ruskins Chambers, Drury Lane, Knutsford, Cheshire WA16
    6HA

Institute of Chartered Accountants (England and Wales),
  Moorgate Place, London EC2

Institute of Chartered Accountants (Scotland),
  24 Holborn, London EC1

Institute of Marketing,
  Moor House, Cookham, Berkshire

Investors in Industry,
  91 Waterloo Road, London SE1 8XP

Law Society,
  113 Chancery Lane, London WC2A 1PL

Manpower Services Commission,
  Moorfoot, Sheffield S1 4PQ

Manpower Society,
  South Stoke, 20 Abbotswood, Guildford, Surrey GU1 1UX

National Chamber of Trade,
  Enterprise House, Henley on Thames, Oxon RG9 1TJ

Market Research Society,
  175 Oxford Street, London W1

Patents Office/Trade Marks Registry,
  25 Southampton Buildings, Chancery Lane, London WC2A
  1AY

Registrar of Business Names (England and Wales),
  Business Registrar, London Chamber of Commerce, 69 Cannon
  Street, London EC4N 5AB

Scottish Development Agency,
  120 Bothwell Street, Glasgow G2 7JP

Small Business Bureau,
  32 Smith Square, London SW1P 3HH

Smaller Firms Council,
  Confederation of British Industry, Centre Point, 103 New
  Oxford Street, London WC1A 1DU

Union of Independent Companies,
  PO Box 186, London SW7 2TF

Welsh Development Agency,
  Pearl House, Greyfriars Road, Cardiff CF1 3XX

Wigan New Enterprise Ltd,
  45 Bridgeman Terrace, Wigan, Lancaster WN1 1TT

NETWORKS

For moral support

Ace UK, the international network for young entrepreneurs,
c/o Business Studies Department, University of Stirling, Stirling
FK9 4LA

Business Graduates Association,
28 Margaret Street, London W1N 7LB

Business Link-Up Ltd,
33 St George Street, London W1R 9FA

Business Opportunities Network, part of the Institute of Small
Business, with a members' monthly digest plus announcements
networking broadsheet,
11 Blomfield Street, London EC2M 7AY

City Women's Network,
58 Coleman Street, London EC2R 5BE

Focus, a resource network for expatriots in the UK,
49 Gower Street, London WC1E 6AR

Homebase, the bimonthly newsletter of the homebased workers to
exchange every sort of opinion/information,
56 London Road, Milborne Port, Sherbourne, Dorset DT9 5DW

In Business in Touch,
Tradewind Magazine, Tynygroes, Conwy, Gwynnedd LL32 8BR

National Women's Register,
245 Warwick Road, Solihull, West Midlands B92 7AH

Network,
25 Park Road, Baker Street, London NW1 6XN

300 Group,
2 The Old Kiln, Nettlebed, Henley on Thames, Oxfordshire

Women in Management Association,
74 Cottenham Park Road, London SW20 0TB

Local Enterprise Agencies for local support groups

Manpower Services Commission, for national directory of
self-employed that have attended their courses

READING

Working From Home – 201 Ways to Make Money, Marianne Gray (Piatkus)

On Our Own, Paul Dickson (Facts on File)

Croner's Reference Book for the Self-Employed and Small Business, Croner Publication

Going Freelance, Godfrey Golzen (Granada)

Essential Law, Dobson, Morris and Rose (Pan Management)

Understand Your Accounts, H, Price (Kogan Page)

Rapid Company Growth: how to plan and manage small company expansion, A. C. Hazell (Business Books)

Be Your Own PR Man, M. Bland (Kogan Page)

How To Collect Money That Is Owed To You, M. Lewis (McGraw-Hill)

Budgetry Control, R. G. A. Boland and David Hall (Hodder & Stoughton)

Marketing Made Simple, B. H. Elvy (W.H. Allen)

Sell Your Way to Success, Alfred Tack (Granada)

The Manual of Sales Promotion, John Williams (Innovation)

Effective Executive, P. Drucker (Pan)

Public Relations, a practical guide, Colin Coulson-Thomas (MacDonald & Evans)

Creative Advertising, David Bernstein (Longman)

Getting Publicity, David Morgan Rees (David & Charley)

Taxation for Small Businesses, J. G. McClure and A. G. Davies (Sphere)

Winners, Robert Bruce (Sidgwick & Jackson)

Routes to Success, Colin Barrow (Kogan Page)

Where to find new products to manufacture, (Intermediate Technology Publications)

Successful Expansion for the Small Business, M. J. Morris (Kogan Page)

The Hidden Persuaders, Vance Packard (Penguin)

INDEX